TEMPERED STEEL

TEMPERED STEEL

HOW GOD SHAPES A MAN'S HEART THROUGH ADVERSITY

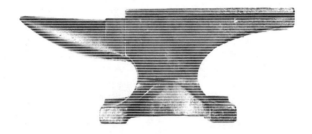

STEVE FARRAR

Multnomah®Publishers *Sisters, Oregon*

TEMPERED STEEL
published by Multnomah Publishers, Inc.

Published in association with the literary agency of Alive Communications, Inc.
7680 Goddard Street, Suite 200, Colorado Springs, CO 80920.

International Standard Book Number: 1-57673-892-2

Cover image by Photodisc
Back cover image by Corbis

Unless otherwise indicated, Scripture quotations are from:
New American Standard Bible © 1960, 1977 by the Lockman Foundation

Other Scripture quotations:
The Holy Bible, New International Version (NIV) © 1973, 1984 by International Bible
Society, used by permission of Zondervan Publishing House
The Holy Bible, King James Version (KJV)
The Message © 1993 by Eugene H. Peterson
Holy Bible, New Living Translation (NLT) © 1996.
Used by permission of Tyndale House Publishers, Inc. All rights reserved.
Revised Standard Version Bible (RSV) © 1946, 1952 by the Division of Christian Education
of the National Council of Churches of Christ in the United States of America.

Multnomah is a trademark of Multnomah Publishers, Inc.,
and is registered in the U.S. Patent and Trademark Office.
The colophon is a trademark of Multnomah Publishers, Inc.

Printed in the United States of America

For information:
MULTNOMAH PUBLISHERS, INC.•POST OFFICE BOX 1720•SISTERS, OREGON 97759

Library of Congress Cataloging-in-Publication Data
Farrar, Steve
Tempered steel / by Steve Farrar.
         p. cm.
Includes bibliographical references.
    ISBN 1-57673-892-2 (pbk.)
  1. Christian men--Religious life. 2. David, King of Israel. 3. David I. Title.
    BV4528.2 .F39 2002
    248.8'42--dc21   2001008460

02 03 04 05 06 07 08—10 9 8 7 6 5 4 3 2 1 0

To Gary Rosberg,
for his friendship that is always
above and beyond the call of duty.

CONTENTS

ACKNOWLEDGMENTS

THERE ARE TWO MEN WHO MADE IT POSSIBLE for you to hold this book in your hands. The first is Don Jacobson. Don is the publisher at Multnomah. I am honored that he puts my stuff in print. If you have read any of my other books, you know that I can get fairly controversial on matters of truth. But Don is a man who is called to put the truth in print. I have seen him do that for years. He backs the truth no matter what it will cost him. It is my privilege to be associated with Don Jacobson.

Larry Libby is my all-time favorite editor. When I pass each chapter off to Larry, I know a little of what Joe Montana must have felt when he threw a pass to Jerry Rice. Somehow, Jerry was going to catch that pass and make the result even better. This is my sixth book with Larry. He has a stout heart for God and an eagle's eye for the right phrase. Larry is the guy who makes this game fun.

INTRODUCTION

AMERICA HAS BEEN BUILT ON STEEL.

Without steel there would be no railroads to crisscross the nation with freight, no interstate highway system to speed us to Grandma's house for Thanksgiving, no cars to speed us along those interstates, and no great river-spanning dams to generate electricity for our homes.

The uses of steel are almost beyond imagination.

Generally speaking, steel is an alloy of iron and carbon. You can't have steel without iron. Iron itself is an alloy. There is a formula for making iron. A recipe. It has been said that making iron is something like baking a cake.[1] The key ingredient in that cake—the "flour," if you will—is iron ore. And into that iron ore you stir coke, limestone, air, and water. This recipe is cooked in a blast furnace that can be as high as fifteen stories, and achieves temperatures up to 3,000 degrees. The intense heat causes the raw materials to melt together. "The melted iron, freed from impurities, trickles down to the lowest part of the furnace….The slag containing the impurities floats on top of iron four or five feet deep."[2]

It takes incredible heat to make iron. But in order to get steel, you need even *more* fire and heat. Steel is stronger than iron, but also flexible, and can be shaped into a number of various products.[3]

There are a number of methods to make steel. One method requires an Open-Hearth furnace—a structure the size of a two-story house, producing temperatures in excess of 3,000 degrees. It is significant that each batch of steel made in a furnace is called a "heat."[4]

Another method is the Bessemer method. The Bessemer converter is an open-topped, egg-shaped furnace that can be tipped on its side. As air is blown into the converter at high pressure, flames shoot into the air with a great roar. These flames reach as high as thirty feet and can be seen for miles at night. The temperatures in the Bessemer method reach up to 3,500 degrees.

Needless to say, there is no steel without fire and heat.

Since the 1850s, some of the most famous steel in the world was Bethlehem Steel. The plants in Bethlehem, Pennsylvania, roared night and day, producing quality steel that found its way all over the world. There was no better steel to be found anywhere than Bethlehem Steel. That small town in the hills of Pennsylvania was known all over the world for the steel that came out of its mills.

I would suggest to you that there is another kind of Bethlehem Steel.

This steel doesn't come from the hills of Pennsylvania, but from a village in the hills just below Jerusalem. It is the steel of soul produced in the lives of men and women who bow to the lordship of Jesus Christ, who was born in Bethlehem. The Lord Jesus Christ not only saves men, He makes and forms men. It is the desire of the Father to conform us into the image of His Son. And like the steel produced in Bethlehem, Pennsylvania, so the tempered steel that God desires to produce in our lives—strong, sure, and flexible—involves tremendous heat and fire.

The Lord Jesus Christ, born as the God-Man in Bethlehem, existed before He was born and placed in a manger. He has always existed. It was He who spoke the worlds into existence. And it was in His Father's plan that a thousand years before the Son would be born to a virgin, another young man would roam the hills of Bethlehem.

David too was born in that little village in the hills. It was God's desire to take this youngest son of Jesse and shape him into a man that could be used for God's glory. There is a process recorded for us in the life of David and in the Psalms. It is the story of a man who was well acquainted with the searing heat of long adversities. Throughout his story you see his impurities coming to the surface. And the reason he was familiar with heat and fire was that God wanted to use him. God wanted to temper him just as God desires to temper us.

There is a process in making steel and there is a process God uses to make a godly man. They are very similar. Do you find yourself in the fire? Do you find yourself in deep pain as your hopes and dreams are burned up before your eyes? You should know that your hardship is not by chance. It is by design. A sovereign design. The God who created you and chose you has something very unique for you to do. But first He must purify you—

allowing the slag to come to the top where it can be skimmed away. That can only occur in the flames and heat of adversity. That may not be a popular message, but it is a true message.

All is not lost if you find yourself in the fire. God is simply getting you ready to fulfill the purpose for which you were created.

As you will see in the pages that follow, you're not alone in those crushing circumstances. You're not by yourself in that furnace.

In fact, you're in the very best of company.

ONE

TRAPDOORS AND PIT STOPS

God works strangely.
He often enriches by impoverishing.

THOMAS WATSON

THERE ARE TWO WAYS TO GET A HOTEL NAMED AFTER YOU.

The first approach is to own the place.

If you can scare up the cash to buy or build a hotel, then you have the right to slap your name over the door. Conrad Hilton built Hilton hotels around the world. J. Willard Marriott did the same with his Marriott chain. That's the first way to get a hotel named after you.

The second method doesn't require cash. It requires greatness.

There is a hotel in Jerusalem that is *the* hotel in Israel—and one of the great hotels in all the world. This hotel has been the meeting place of diplomats and CEOs from every corner of the planet. Under its roof, three different governments in exile have headquartered themselves at various times throughout the twentieth century. Just last fall, in a single evening, an incoming president of the United States, two former presidents, the U.S. secretary of state and a number of former secretaries of state, the prime minister of Britain, the heir to the British throne, the king and queen of Jordan, and the president of Egypt were all sleeping under its roof.[1]

I do not refer to the Jerusalem Red Roof Inn.

This elite and prestigious establishment is known as the King David Hotel.

When David was a teenager, minding his father's sheep in the hills around Bethlehem, he had no idea that one day, three thousand years in the future, the leaders of the world would stay in a great inn, just a few miles away, that would bear his name.

But that's precisely what happened.

David went through some major transitions to get from the obscurity of being a shepherd to the throne of Israel. Everyone goes through transitions. Change is part of life. You've been through it and so have I. But let's be honest about it: Some transitions are tougher than others.

The toughest transitions are what I call *trapdoor* transitions.

A DOOR IN THE FLOOR

Have you ever seen an old movie where some character falls through a trapdoor in the floor? He's walking through some winding castle hallway, minding his own business, when he steps on a portion of the flooring and—*whoosh!*— he suddenly disappears, plunging into some dark, cobwebby tunnel or dungeon.

Maybe you've experienced something similar in your life. Your world seems to be spinning along in a normal fashion, you're going about your affairs just like you do every day, and then—*bam!* All of a sudden there's thin air beneath you where the floor ought to be. You know exactly what I'm talking about, don't you? You've experienced the trapdoors and so have I. Totally unforeseen and completely unexpected, trapdoors have a way of radically changing your life in the blink of an eye. That's what happens when the bottom falls out.

We remember Winston Churchill as perhaps the greatest prime minister in the history of Great Britain. By the steel of his will, he led his island nation to stand against Hitler and eventually triumph in World War II. But years before that victorious moment for the ages, Churchill found himself plunging through a succession of devastating trapdoors—each one worse than the last.

In August of 1929, Churchill had managed to bring in approximately $70,000 into the family coffers. That's a lot of money even today. In 1929 it was an unimaginable amount for a single month's work. He invested nearly all of it in the American stock market. He then jotted a note to his wife saying how pleased he was to finally reach a place of financial independence. Less than ninety days later the stock market fell through its own trapdoor and Churchill lost virtually everything.

It was a major blow. Churchill had experienced ninety days of financial security—and then the bottom fell out. For the first time in his adult life he'd been on easy street, enjoying the prospects of a comfortable future, and then—whoosh! bam!—the trapdoor fell open beneath his feet and down he went.

That setback alone would be enough to send most any man deep down into the dungeon of depression. But there were two more trapdoors that waited quietly and patiently for Churchill to arrive. In 1931, after serving his entire adult life as a central figure in the British government, he was not invited to serve in the cabinet. This was another staggering blow to Churchill. He had been banished to the political wilderness. While Hitler was working full-time to build his war machine, Churchill, virtually the only British politician who saw the reality of Hitler's threat, was put out to pasture. When he should have been on center stage, he was banished to his country home where he wrote, painted, built brick walls, and cleaned out ponds to keep himself busy. The great statesman was sent down to the minors to play Class A ball when he should have been starting in the All-Star game. This defeat was even more bitter than his financial loss.

It was heating up in that British steel furnace.

And then in the same year, while he was trying to hold things together financially and fight off the depression of political defeat, he decided to take a tour of Canada and the United States. In New York City he looked the wrong way before crossing a street and was hit by a taxi traveling at thirty-five miles per hour. The accident sent him to the hospital, clinging to life by a thread.

In less than three years he had suffered three shattering trapdoor transitions; devastating him financially, then politically, and then in an accident that nearly cost him his life. In a letter to their son from the hospital, his wife wrote: "Last night he was very sad and said he had now in the last two years had three very heavy blows. First the loss of all that money in the crash, the loss of political position in the Conservative Party and now this terrible injury. He said he did not think he would ever recover completely from the three events."[2]

At that point, as he convalesced in that New York hospital room, Churchill was fifty-seven years old. Eventually he did recover from all three trapdoors. Nine years later, at the right moment in history, the government that had ignored him would turn to him in desperation.

But he couldn't see that future as he lay in that hospital bed.

All he could see were the three trapdoors that had taken nearly everything away from him. In fact, Churchill's prospects looked so dismal at that moment that one of his enemies was emboldened enough to pronounce a political eulogy: "Churchill," he said, "is finished."

Famous last words! History proved that statement to be just a tad premature.

Perhaps, like Churchill, you have experienced some devastating losses and reversals. You feel like the heat and stress from a dozen pressing circumstances are slowly bending you out of shape. And the thought has crossed your mind that you will never be able to recover. There might even be some critics who are writing you off as finished...and you're beginning to think they may be right.

Trapdoors can do that to a man. Those sudden, floor-dropping moments can take away our finances, our careers, and our health. They can take away our carefully laid plans and strategies. They can rob us of our marriages and our most important friendships. That's precisely why trapdoor transitions are so devastating.

But God is bigger than the trapdoors that suddenly send us into free-fall dives without a parachute. And to be quite honest about it, those trapdoors are there by His design and with His permission. That statement may puzzle and confuse you. It deserves some backup—and I promise you we'll get to that very soon. But we left David back with the sheep. And to understand what is happening in your life, we need to take a quick scan of the trapdoor transitions that sent David's life reeling.

DAVID LEFT TRACKS

Like Churchill, David was no stranger to sudden reversals. The events of David's life have been chronicled for us in the book of Psalms. Do you know why the Psalms ring true and bring such comfort to us? Because many of us have experienced the very same sorts of trapdoor transitions that David penned into his journal—events like betrayal, depression, financial reversals, family difficulties, and the consequences of poor personal decisions.

David wrote approximately half of the book of Psalms. As a result, you can easily see how the lines of those Hebrew poems weave their way in and through the events of David's life.

In other words, David left tracks. We can follow the trail he walked through the books of Kings and Chronicles. He points us to the faithfulness of God when life knocks us out of the saddle.

While still a young man, David tasted difficulty, disappointment, discouragement, and defeat. For a brief season of his life, he had felt the fresh, exhilarating wind on the mountain heights of accomplishment, but he also knew all about those black swamps of depression.

David often referred to "the path" in the Psalms. A path is a trail, as is the Christian life. But fortunately, it is a marked trail. David, under the inspiration of the Holy Spirit, marked the trail that he was on as he pursued the Lord across the peaks and valleys. That marked trail is recorded for us in the Psalms—and that is why we go so quickly to the book of Psalms when life becomes confusing and difficult.

It makes sense, doesn't it? In the pages of the Psalms we find that the trail has been marked by those who have gone before. And we find ourselves climbing the same hills, staring into the depths of the same, starry heavens, and wading through the same murky swamps that David experienced three thousand years ago.

There is a trail. There is a path God has designed ahead of time for you to walk in. He has a plan for you.

I know…that's just a little difficult to believe sometimes.

We get frustrated. We experience major setbacks. We struggle through deep disappointments. We don't like to admit it, but sometimes our hearts get broken. Sometimes we find ourselves stuck—stuck in our careers, stuck in our marriages, stuck in the same old personal habits. Quite frankly, at times we feel trapped; trapped by circumstances, trapped by our finances, trapped by our failures, trapped because we've hit the ceiling in our careers. And we think there is no escape.

I'm thinking of two Christian men who became so overwhelmed by their circumstances that they committed suicide. That was their way of dealing with crushing adversity; they decided to pull the trapdoor on their own lives. Evidently, in their despair and loss of perspective, they decided to take what seemed at the time to be the easy way out. And in doing so, they yanked the floorboards out from under everyone else in their families. They left quite a mess for someone else to clean up.

This trail has its ups and downs, and David tracked through every one of them. But you've got to hand it to him. Every time he got knocked down, he got right back up. He didn't *stay* down. He resisted the urge to quit. He refused the urge to just chuck it all.

Before he was twenty, David, the future king of Israel, went through two major transitions. The first was your typical rags-to-riches success story. The second was a trapdoor. But I'm getting ahead of myself. Let's go back to the trailhead and chart David's amazing story from the beginning.

Rags-to-Riches

David's journey reminds us of a good old poor-boy-makes-the-big-time American success story. Only it didn't happen in America; it happened in Israel about three thousand years ago. At first the temptation is to think that this story, fascinating and intriguing as it may be, really has no application to or bearing on your life. But making that assumption would be a serious mistake. Unless I miss my guess, this story will speak profoundly and precisely to your personal life and circumstances.

David was minding his own business. The youngest brother of a good-sized clan, he led a life of obscurity and loneliness as he took care of his dad's sheep. David was just a teenager—somewhere between sixteen and twenty years old—and had been watching over those woollies for a number of years. As far as he knew, he was going to be a shepherd for the rest of his life. Oh, sure, maybe he'd do a couple-year hitch in the army, but then it would probably be right back to the flocks.

It wasn't that bad of a life. The Bible gives no indication that David was discontented with his lot. Every now and then he would have to go one-on-

one with a lion or a bear, but other than that it was a fairly quiet, low-stress lifestyle. Sure, there was lots of solitude. But that gave David plenty of time to practice with his slingshot, work on his music, and develop his friendship with the living God. Young men didn't have a lot of options in Israel three thousand years ago, and realistically, David could look forward to a life of working in the family business and expanding Jesse's flock of sheep.

Then one day he got word that his father wanted to see him back at the ranch house. He walked in and there stood his dad, his seven older brothers, and…Samuel, *the prophet and judge of Israel.* That would be like coming home for dinner with the family and finding Billy Graham at your kitchen table, sipping an iced tea in his stocking feet. David took one look at Samuel and knew something was up.

And something *was* up.

Before David could get his bearings, he was kneeling before the old prophet with the anointing oil streaming down his face and neck. Samuel told him that God had chosen him to be *the next king of Israel.*

You've heard of sticker shock? This was *anointing* shock. Who was he that God would reach down and choose him to be king of Israel? He was just a kid; just a simple young shepherd with sheep dung on his sandals. And God was going to elevate him from a shepherd to a king? That's what you call major-league change.

Psalm 78:70–71 describes this stunning transition. I quote this verse as rendered in The Message:

> Then he [God] chose David, his servant,
>   handpicked him from his work in the sheep pens.
> One day he was caring for the ewes and their lambs,
>   the next day God had him shepherding Jacob,
>   his people, Israel, his prize possession.

The word that comes to my mind here is *transition*. You've had some big transitions in your life and so have I, but going from the sheep pens to the palace is like a missile launch.

But here's the catch. This anointing was secret. Saul, of course, was already on the throne as king of Israel—and fully inclined to stay there. David was to succeed Saul as king, but the question of *when* that was supposed to happen hadn't been revealed yet. Until God chose to make it known, knowledge of this anointing of David would remain under lock and key.

In spite of the fact that no one other than his family was aware that he'd been chosen to be the next king of Israel, David's life began an immediate transition.

King Saul was being tormented by evil spirits because the Spirit of God had left him, and the only thing that would soothe him was music. Someone in his inner circle (who was probably anxious for Saul to mellow out) mentioned that there was this shepherd kid in Bethlehem who played a pretty mean harp. And that's when Saul—completely unaware of the fact that Jesse's youngest son was God's handpicked successor for his job—summoned David to a gig in the king's private quarters.

David went back and forth from his home in Bethlehem to play music for Saul. He was the court musician, and before long, he was promoted again to be Saul's armor bearer. That was quite an opportunity for a teenage shepherd from the hill country. But not long after that, something else developed that would change David's life forever.

RICHES-TO-RAGS

Jesse told David to take some food to his brothers, who were in the Israeli army, and see how they were doing. As David approached their camp, his eyes fell on the biggest man he had ever seen in his life on the other side of a ravine. It was Goliath, belching out challenges to the Jews to come and fight him, mocking and blaspheming them and their God.

You know the rest of the story.

David was incensed by this huge goon who had intimidated the army of Israel and slurred the name of God. David went out to confront him, and with one well-placed stone from his sling, Goliath was permanently out of the picture.

Saul was thrilled that this monster Philistine had been defeated and beheaded by David. Out of gratitude, he gave his daughter Michal to be David's wife. "After that, there was no stopping David's rise to fame. Soon the former shepherd was leading a thousand men into battle, enjoying such phenomenal military success that all Israel was singing his praises."[3]

So far, so good. The kid was on a roll. In a very short period of time he had racked up some major successes. Life was good. He had gone very quickly from the pasture to the inner circle of Israel's elite. He was married to the king's daughter, enjoyed the favor of all the people, and seemed to be on the fast track to success. The Bible declares, "In everything he did he had great success, because the LORD was with him" (1 Samuel 18:14, NIV). Overnight, he had become a national hero. They were even writing songs about him!

And that is the particular moment when the trapdoor opened without warning beneath David's sandals and everything came crashing down.

When King Saul heard that the people were singing, "Saul has slain his thousands, and David his tens of thousands," he lost it. The king went into a jealous, insane rage and tried to kill David with his spear. From then on—and for many weary years to follow—David would be a man on the run.

David was a fugitive for the next ten, maybe twelve years of his life. Yes, he was eventually going to replace Saul. But he wouldn't realize that promotion for a long, long time. He'd had a small taste of life in the palace. He'd sampled the fine wine and enjoyed the great dinners and privileges. For a kid who was used to hanging out with sheep, that was quite a transition. But that transition was nothing compared to the transition that occurred when Saul sprung the trapdoor and threw David into an era of great personal pain and darkness.

> Trouble and heartache roared into David's life like a flood. In short order, he lost his job, was driven from his wife and home, was separated from his best friend, and was forced to flee to the wilderness for his very life. The same army he had previously led in triumph only a few months earlier was now pursuing him as Public Enemy Number One.... David lived the life of a fugitive constantly on the move; constantly in danger of capture and execution; running from one place to the next; hiding in lonely forests or lurking in limestone caves. [4]

That long chapter of David's life was filled with fear, anxiety, and the constant danger that he would be found and killed. In other words, when the bottom dropped out under David's feet, he was in a free fall for a long, long time. That's what a trapdoor can do to you.

Are you enjoying a season of success right now? That's great. Thank the Lord. But here's a word of caution about success. Don't count on it. Don't bank on it. And above all, don't trust in it. It could be gone tomorrow. Just ask David. You need something greater and bigger than success to build your life upon.

PIT STOPS

The Bible never uses the term *trapdoor.* But it does use the word *pit.* And that term *pit* is very, very appropriate. For when a trapdoor is suddenly sprung beneath you, you find yourself taking an unplanned swan dive governed only by the law of gravity. Shocked, stunned, and out of control; you're headed down like a wounded P-51 in a World War II dogfight. And where will you land?

You will land in the pit.

That's where young Joseph landed when his older brothers pulled the trapdoor on his life (Genesis 37:24).

When the bottom dropped out of Job's life he too was headed for the pit.

Jonah, in his refusal to obey the Lord's clear direction, wound up in a semi-liquid pit (Jonah 2:6).

The weeping prophet, Jeremiah, called out to the Lord from the lowest pit (Lamentations 3:55). At one point, the prophet was in the pit up to his arm pits. (Jeremiah 38:6–13).

It was not uncommon in Old Testament days for a man to dig a pit for the express purpose of trapping his enemy, covering up the hole with brush and dirt for camouflage. Often they would stretch a net on the floor of the pit and up along the walls with the top ends well hidden under the brush. If the man who built the pit was successful, it would trap his enemy and render him helpless. When his captors came to get him, they would simply pull him up in the net.

Here's a short sampling of some "pit" verses:

He has dug a pit and hollowed it out,
And has fallen into the hole which he made. (Psalm 7:15)

That nations have sunk down in the pit which they have made;
In the net which they hid, their own foot has been caught.
   (Psalm 9:15)

He who digs a pit will fall into it,
And he who rolls a stone, it will come back on him.
   (Proverbs 26:27)

He who leads the upright astray in an evil way
Will himself fall into his own pit,
But the blameless will inherit good. (Proverbs 28:10)

He who digs a pit may fall into it, and a serpent may bite him who breaks through a wall. (Ecclesiastes 10:8)

The pits were the Old Testament equivalent of a trapdoor. You've heard the term *pitfall?* It comes right out of the Old Testament. If the pit was dug and camouflaged successfully, someone was going to fall into that pit.

When Saul pulled the lever on the trapdoor that lunged David out of the palace for the next ten or twelve years of his life, it looked to some outsiders like God had abandoned the son of Jesse. But nothing could have been further from the truth.

For over ten years, Saul had an all points bulletin out on David. Saul had his intelligence network and his undercover informants looking for David from one end of the country to the other. David was a fugitive with a price on his head. And this was no TV show or movie. It was real life.

Amazingly enough, David took time to write at least three magnificent psalms while he was on the run from Saul. He penned these heartfelt songs while hiding in the caves and the surrounding wilderness: Psalms 54, 57, and 63. In Psalm 57:6, David states very clearly that Saul is trying to force him into the pit. David was already in a pit of desperate and difficult circumstances, but Saul was trying to force him into a snare that would cost him his life. Thousands of soldiers were scouring the hills, canyons, and caves looking for the former war hero, and it was all David could do to keep a step ahead of them. They were hell-bent on killing him.

When you're hiding out in the caves as David was, you are *literally* in the pit. It just happens to be horizontal instead of vertical. But no matter what shape of a pit you're in, no matter what the particular configurations of the hole in which you find yourself, the question that is always simmering on the back burner of your mind is, "How will I ever get out of this?" Or to put it another way, "How will I ever get *through* this?"

GETTING THROUGH

When we find ourselves in our own personal pits, when we find the heat of adversity beginning to sear us to the melting point, the issue is always getting through.

Pits don't all look the same. Everyone's pit is a little different.

Some pits are in a hospital. Your wife or your child is in a bed, surrounded by IVs, tubes, and monitors. Like the guy I talked to last week on the West Coast whose five-year-old son has brain cancer. One day he had a healthy, energetic son, and the next day the bottom dropped out. And that trapdoor transitioned his family right into a hospital. As he sits in the room night after night, praying for his son, I'm sure he wonders quite often: *How in the world will we ever get through this?*

Or the guy in his late forties who has successfully climbed the professional ladder in his career. He's got two kids in college, a big mortgage, and enough financial pressure on his shoulders to flatten a Sherman tank. And last month he was laid off along with six thousand of his co-workers—another trapdoor transition. Two years ago his stock options were climbing into the wild-blue like an F-16. But now they've got about as much value as a collapsed tent. He's made all the phone calls and pulled all the strings. But nobody's hiring. And at three o'clock in the morning, nearly every morning, while his wife and kids are sleeping, he's wondering: *How will I ever get through this?*

Another guy's wife just left him for a man she met over the Internet. She's walking out on him and the three kids. She's leaving for la-la land, and her family is in free fall—all sense of security and trust scattered like leaves in the wind. And her husband is asking: *How in the world will I ever get through this?*

Theodore Roosevelt was one of the greatest presidents in American history. He was a man who passionately loved God, loved the Bible, and loved his country. He had the vision to cut a canal through the Isthmus of Panama and the guts to lead a charge up San Juan Hill. He had many accomplishments and victories. But he also experienced numerous trapdoors that put him in the pit.

On what should have been the greatest night of his life, tragedy struck. His wife had just presented him with a beautiful baby girl. But even as he held his newborn little girl, his wife began to take a turn for the worse. Her vital signs began to dramatically diminish. Incredibly, in another room in the same house, Theodore's mother suddenly became deathly ill. She had been fighting a cold, but in a matter of hours, she too was fighting for her life. The doctor realized she had an advanced stage of typhoid fever. Theodore Roosevelt would go from the joy of holding his daughter to the depths of despair as he would look in on his mother. Then he would sink even further into depression as he would go into the room of his wife. Just several days after his daughter's birth, his mother died. Within hours, his young pretty wife, Alice, followed her into eternity at the age of twenty-two. In a matter of two days, to use his own words, "the light went out of his life." Theodore Roosevelt was deep in the pit.

Can you imagine such a night? In the same twenty-four hour period the two women he loved most passed into eternity. And I'm sure that in the stillness of the gray dawn, as he rocked his baby girl, he thought to himself: *How will I ever get through this?*

A son on drugs will put you in the pit. So will a failed business. Finding out that your daughter has been living a double life will send you to the depths in a heartbeat.

Sometimes we dig our own pits. I'm thinking of a man who is trying to rebuild trust with his wife after a three-year affair. To his credit, he's trying to do the right thing. But he's in a very deep pit because his wife has completely lost trust in him. Understandably so! He betrayed her. He's going to be in that pit for quite a while. You don't rebuild trust overnight. It takes time— lots of time—to regain trust after it has been squandered.

Whatever your circumstances, there is one surefire way to know that you are in the pit. Perhaps you know you are in the pit when you ask over and over again: *How will I ever get through this?*

UNSCHEDULED PIT STOPS

David was a man after God's own heart. He followed the path God had set before him. You and I are on that very same trail. And that's why, sooner or later, we're going to experience our own personal pits, just as David did.

Just as the bottom drops out and we begin to career head over heels into that deep, dark crater, we may take a quick look around and notice that everyone else seems to be cruising along and enjoying life. As they say in Australia, "no worries." But that simply isn't true. (In fact, Australia has one of the highest suicide rates in the world.) There is no one who escapes the pits as they walk along the trail of life. The fact of the matter is that there are people all around you who are in the pit *right now.* It just doesn't look that way from your perspective.

It's a hard trail that we're on. Some guys find themselves in the pit of alcohol; others deal with the pit of failing health—or maybe prolonged unemployment. But none of us can manage to completely avoid those hidden holes in the ground. Pit stops are inevitable.

I have noticed that these pit stops are almost always *unscheduled.* We have our dreams, plans, hopes, and ambitions. We're working hard to accomplish our dreams, and then suddenly—*whoosh! bam!* The floor disappears beneath our feet and we're on the express bus into the pit. Unscheduled pit stops derail our plans and time tables.

Churchill had a plan for financial independence, but he took an unscheduled pit stop that put an end to his plan for a good many years. I don't know about you, but I don't have *time* for those sorts of pit stops. They put my life behind schedule—and life is passing by. Have you ever felt that way? Sure you have.

May I offer another perspective? That pit stop may have been unscheduled from your perspective, but from God's viewpoint it was scheduled all along. That trapdoor transition may have been a surprise to you, but it was no surprise to the Lord. He knew about it from before the foundations of the earth.

And that's why your time in the pit is not putting you behind schedule.

It may be putting you behind *your* schedule, but not His. Vance Havner said it best, "He who waits on God loses no time."

Unscheduled pit stops are tough. Especially when they linger on and there is no hope on the horizon that anything is going to change.

Remember Job? He was a wealthy, godly man. He is described as blameless, upright, fearing God, and turning away from evil. He was above reproach in reputation and character. He had vast holdings and wealth. He had a full quiver of children—seven sons and three daughters—who delighted his heart. He had a spread that would knock your socks off: 7000 sheep, 3000 camels, 500 yoke of oxen, 500 female donkeys, and enough servants and farmhands to take care of the whole she-bang. The Bible says that he was the greatest of all the men of the East. Quite frankly, Job had it made. He had wealth, health, and a bright future. And then one day—*whoosh! bam!*—he fell into the biggest pit this side of Uz. In one swift moment, a freight train of bad news blasted through his once-tranquil life.

His enemies had attacked, stealing his oxen and donkeys and killing his servants. What a blow! But he'd hardly had time to absorb that news when another report came in that all of his sheep had been destroyed—along with their shepherds. While the servant was still giving this report, a third servant came running in and reported that the camels had been stolen and, once again, all of the servants tending them had been brutally killed. No sooner had that report been given than the news came that all of his children had been killed as they dined together in the home of the eldest brother. The roof had caved in, and there were no survivors.

> Then Job arose and tore his robe and shaved his head, and he fell to
>   the ground and worshiped.
> He said, "Naked I came from my mother's womb,
> And naked I shall return there.
> The LORD gave and the LORD has taken away.
> Blessed be the name of the LORD."
> Through all this Job did not sin nor did he blame God.
> (Job 1:20–22)

Somehow, I don't think that would have been my reaction.

But it was certainly Job's.

On this particular day, in a matter of minutes, Job lost everything dear to him. He was in the biggest trapdoor transition of his entire life. He was officially in the pit. And there's no question that, for Job, it was an unscheduled pit stop.

Job made a remarkable statement about God after these calamities took place, and I turn to the old Puritan writer Thomas Watson for his observation on Job's response.

> "Job eyed God in his affliction; therefore, as Augustine observed, he does not say, 'The Lord gave, and the devil took away,' but, 'The Lord hath taken away.' Whoever brings an affliction to us, it is God that sends it."[5]

Did you catch that? Job didn't say, "The Lord gives but Satan has taken away." Rather, he laid it out this way, "The Lord gives and the Lord takes away, blessed be the name of the Lord."

If you read the book of Job carefully, you will discover that Satan asked permission to afflict Job's well-being. And God granted permission to show Satan the true condition of Job's heart. Yes, Satan was involved in Job's distress, but Job knew that God Himself had permitted that trapdoor to swing open. Ultimately, it was the Lord who had inflicted his loss. Thomas Watson wisely writes, "instruments can no more stir till God gives them a commission, than the axe can cut of itself without a hand.[6]

That is a perspective we rarely hear in our day. I have pulled these observations of Thomas Watson's from a book that he wrote in 1633. The book is entitled *All Things for Good*. The title is a reference to Romans 8:28:

> And we know that God causes all things to work together for good to those who love God, to those who are called according to His purpose.

The first chapter of Watson's book is called "The Best Things Work for Good to the Godly." The second chapter is "The Worst Things Work for Good to the Godly."

It was a tragic day when the people of Judah were yanked out of Jerusalem and slapped into captivity in Babylon. They lost their homes, their families, their culture, their temple, and their language. They lost everything. Among these exiles was Daniel, a teenager at the time. What a devastating calamity! Yet the Scriptures say in Jeremiah 24:5:

> Like these good figs, so will I acknowledge them that are carried away captive of Judah, whom I have sent out of this place into the land of the Chaldeans [Babylonians], *for their good.* (KJV, emphasis added)

Daniel and his fellow Jews grieved over their captivity. But God declared He did it for their good.

In Psalm 119:71, after going through a devastating experience of hardship, the psalmist declared, "It [was] good for me that I was afflicted."

So what are we saying here?

We are saying that when the trapdoor opens and throws you down into an unscheduled stop, no matter how painful and how bitter that pit may be, God is absolutely in charge of your life. And ultimately, He is the one who has put you there. As much as you may hate and despise the pain and heartache of your pit, God has put you there for your good. That doesn't mean that what is happening is good. Cancer is not good; divorce is not good. But God is bigger than any pit and will turn it for your good.

Corrie ten Boom might have said it best. Reflecting on her nightmare life in a Nazi concentration camp, she wrote: "No matter how deep our darkness, God is deeper still."

Nobody in his right mind likes being in the pit. If you enjoyed it, it wouldn't be a pit. Joseph didn't like the pit, and neither did Job. Jeremiah hated the pit, and so did David.

But may I remind you of something about these men? God didn't leave them in the pit. Ultimately, he delivered every one of them.

Have you begun to imagine in your heart that you will never get out of your pit? I'm sure that Joseph and Jonah, Job and David, all had days when they had to fight off despair. Are you on the verge of despair? Has that trapdoor thrown you down so deep that you think you will never get out?

Sometimes we lose hope…we tell ourselves that life will always be this way. If the truth were known, at times we have completely lost our joy. The only "joy" that comes across our path is the stuff our wife squirts in the kitchen sink. Other than that, joy is something way, way back on our trail. It's been years since we've known anything of personal joy.

So what do you do during those times of drudgery and hopelessness? Is there any hope? Is there a purpose in those trials God has allowed to come into your life?

You bet there is.

God has designed those hardships to make you a better man. That's the real reason you are in the pit. He wants to bend you and shape you and form you through the heat of adversity. He wants to conform you to the image of Christ.

God used Winston Churchill to defend Christian civilization against the demonic teaching and violence of Hitler. So Churchill had to go through the pit. God used Joseph to oversee a crisis of worldwide proportions. So Joseph had to go through the pit. God wanted to use Job as an example of His goodness and mercy that would endure for millennia, finally restoring to him double everything he had lost. So Job had to go through the pit. God had plans to bless David not only in his lifetime, but for eternity. So David had to go through the pit.

Are you in the pit? God is preparing to do something great in your life. No, you probably can't see it when you're in the pit. But He sees it. So stay teachable and obedient. Yield your will to His. He knows what He's doing. And as bad as things may seem, you are right on schedule. At the right time, He will bring you out of the pit. He will bring good into your life. What will He do? Only He knows. Maybe someday, someone will name a hotel after you.

But I have a feeling it's going to be much better than that.

TWO

THIS IS A TEST

Great hearts can only be made through great troubles.

C. H. SPURGEON

MICHAEL LEWIS TELLS THE STORY OF A MAN WHO VISITED New College in Oxford, England. Actually, this "new" college wasn't new at all. As he walked into the College Commons building, he asked when it had been constructed.

"1386," the administrator replied.

As the visitor looked around at the weathered and stately old structure, his eyes were drawn to the majestic oak beams that crisscrossed and buttressed the open ceiling. He'd never seen anything like them. They were huge, massive, and magnificent.

He asked if those were the original beams.

"No, they're not. They were replaced in the late 1890s. Those are the new beams."

Those "new beams" were well over a hundred years old. The administrator continued with his story. "When it became apparent, in the 1890s, that the original beams were in need of replacement, a small crisis developed. No one knew where they would ever be able to find giant oaks of the size that could yield such massive replacement beams. It was the college forester who provided the answer.

"Hidden away in the back hills of the college property, is a great stand of giant oaks. Those oaks are over 550 years old. Interestingly enough, they were all planted at the same time, by the same man. And the man who planted those oaks is the same man who fashioned and raised the original beams back in 1386."

That story, whose origin may be somewhat apocryphal, yields a tremendous truth. The man who crafted and raised the original beams knew that their strength and usefulness would face the test of time. Those great beams would last for centuries. And, at some point—four, five, or even six hundred years in the future—they would begin to fail the test. They would be tried in the balance and fall short. The test of the ages would eventually wear them down.

Knowing that one day they would no longer be able to pass the test, the designer had the vision and foresight to plant their very stand-ins.

In Psalm 11:4-5, David writes:

> The LORD is in His holy temple; the LORD's throne is in heaven;
> His eyes behold, His eyelids test the sons of men.
> The LORD tests the righteous and the wicked....

As the great beams were tested by the weight of the ceiling above it, we too will be tested by the Lord. God is more interested in great hearts than He is in great beams, and as C. H. Spurgeon put it, "Great hearts can only be made through great troubles."

PIT UNIVERSITY

David knew what it was to be tested by God in his own life. He knew what it was to be in a pit of great trouble. There were many pits throughout David's life, some the result of normal life circumstances, and others the result of his own poor judgment and sin. Whatever the reason for his troubles, David knew that those troubles were a kind of testing. And the same is true for you and me.

David is described as "a man after God's own heart." He had a great heart in the midst of great troubles. Sure, David had his failures. But in the midst of every pit of testing, David's heart for God shone through. He loved his Lord in the good times and in the tough times.

David developed his heart for God as a young boy, watching over his father's sheep. No one had ever heard of him or his heroic exploits in defending the flock against the lion and the bear. But God knew about David. And more importantly, God saw David's heart. A young man who would risk his own life for his sheep—even to the point of taking on a lion or a bear—could be trusted to shepherd God's own people.

In time, Samuel would arrive at Jesse's ranch and anoint David to be the second king of Israel. But don't let this fact escape your notice: David was tested before he was promoted.

In the last chapter, we saw that as David came to the attention of Saul, the king turned with jealousy against the young man. David became a fugitive who had to run for his life. What a huge pit of trouble for the future king of Israel! It was a pit that tested him in the deepest parts of his life. This pit lasted for nearly ten years.

That is a very long test—a long course of study at Pit University. But David passed the test. That's not to imply that he was the model of perfection during this time of his life. He wasn't. He took multiple wives when God had forbidden it (Deuteronomy 17:17). Don't get the idea that David had straight A's in this test, because he didn't. But God is a God of grace and mercy. He is good and gracious to us in spite of our flaws. God is looking for a right heart, not an impeccable life. Once again, he saw the heart of David in this prolonged and trouble-filled pit. And finally, at the age of thirty, David assumed the throne of Israel.

When David became king, he hit the ground running. He had a tremendous start right out of the blocks. David's biography in the book of 2 Samuel outlines for us the trail that he walked on this earth. After reviewing David's bio, F. B. Meyer made a tremendous observation:

In the first ten chapters of 2 Samuel, David could do no wrong. He is never defeated in battle. Never wrong in judgment. He begins his reign in prayer and continues in faith. Enemies are subdued, the nation is unified, the capital secured, and the boundary extends from six thousand to sixty thousand square miles....But that is the first ten chapters.[1]

And then one night, in chapter 11, David found himself on his rooftop, watching Bathsheba get into her Jacuzzi. This was a test; a test David failed. Instead of turning away from sin, David turned to pursue it and fell into the biggest pit of his life. What made this pit so bitter was that it was one he had dug for himself.

> Storm clouds of shame, anguish, and violence darken the remaining years of David's life. The king's sorrows begin when he yields to the double sins of adultery and murder. Confronted by God's word through Nathan the prophet, David repents and is forgiven by the Lord. Consequences of David's sin, however, fill his remaining years with strife. Incest, murder, and rebellion tear at the king's family— and break the king's heart.
>
> The cruelest blow of all comes when David's handsome and gifted son Absalom stages a coup, forcing his father into exile. Although Absalom is killed and David is restored to the throne, the king is consumed by grief for his son. [2]

David knew what it was to be in the pit. But these pits, painful as they were, matured and refined him into a better man. Every pit brings about a test—even if it is of our own making. God can and will use anything to conform us to the image of Christ. Yes, He can use even the consequences of personal failure to accomplish His work in the deepest recesses of our hearts. Many of the psalms reflect the deep tests that David went through as he found himself in the pit.

You'll recall that that's why Psalms is the first place so many of us turn to when we find ourselves tested in the pit of hard circumstances and personal failure. David has walked that same trail before us, and he marked that trail in the book of Psalms. That's why we so quickly identify with David. He has been where we are now!

No man that God wants to build will be exempt from testing. For testing is the steel furnace that our good and wise God has chosen to bend and shape men for His glory.

TESTED THROUGH AND THROUGH

I started school when I was four and finished when I was thirty-nine. That's the way it works when you're a slow learner.

I've done a little bit of calculating, and I figure that in my twenty-five years or so of school, I have taken over three thousand tests. That's a lot of tests. Quite frankly, I'm a little bit tired of taking tests. That's why I got a little testy (pun intended) when I went to get my driver's license renewed and the lady told me I needed to take a driving test. After three thousand tests, I'm sort of tested out.

As I look back over all those tests, each one falls into one of two categories. The first is what I call a *premeditated* test. This would include both midterm and final exams, as well as any other tests the teacher tells you about in advance. In most college courses, on the very first day of class the professor hands out a syllabus of the course, detailing the dates of both the midterm and the final, even though they are weeks away. You see, the professor has thought about these tests in advance. And more importantly, he has warned you that they're coming.

But as difficult as premeditated tests may be, there is another type of test that is worse by far. Perhaps it's been a beautiful fall weekend, and you spent those short, glorious days between Friday and Monday having a great time with your friends. Your team won the football game on Saturday afternoon, you saw a good movie on Saturday night, and you spent Sunday after church riding up to the lake and getting in a few final hours of waterskiing before the warm sun disappeared until spring. What a weekend! What great weather!

You hated to get up on Monday and go to class, but there you are. As you wait for the professor to show up, you gaze out the window, remembering that golden weekend, wishing it could go on and on and....

Suddenly, the voice of your professor knifes into your reverie. "Good morning. I want you to put away your books and please take out a pen and a piece of paper."

A gasp runs through the class. Oh no! The worst of all possible scenarios has come true. You are about to undergo the most brutal form of testing ever conceived by educational bureaucrats. You are now going to have a *pop quiz*.

Upon hearing that dreaded news, I can remember breathing a swift, desperate prayer: *Lord, bring to my mind things I have never read!*

At that point, I am in major-league trouble. Yes, it's true that the prof gave a reading assignment for the weekend—but he never mentioned anything about a *test*. This is the world of the pop quiz. A pop quiz is a sudden, unannounced examination designed to determine your understanding of a particular subject. Note the two words *sudden* and *unannounced*.

Therein lies the difficulty.

Pop quizzes are the worst possible form of testing because they come without warning.

ALL I REALLY NEEDED TO KNOW ABOUT TESTING, I LEARNED IN THE NEW TESTAMENT

Unfortunately, tests don't come to an end when we finally finish clawing our way up the educational ladder. For those of us who enjoy a personal relationship with Jesus Christ, testing is a fairly normal part of the Christian life. James, the half-brother of Jesus, described testing in this way:

> Consider it all joy, my brethren, when you encounter various trials, knowing that the *testing* of your faith produces endurance. (James 1:2–3, emphasis added)

That's another way of saying, "The heat of adversity will temper the steel of your soul and make you strong."

Peter also had some appropriate words on testing:

> In this you greatly rejoice, even though now for a little while, if necessary, you have been distressed by various trials, so that the proof of your faith, being more precious than gold which is perishable, even though *tested* by fire, may be found to result in praise and glory and honor at the revelation of Jesus Christ. (1 Peter 1:6–7, emphasis added)

It is fairly obvious from these verses that testing is a major part of the Christian life. But have you ever asked yourself what *kind* of testing James and Peter are talking about? I've had my faith tested a number of times, as

I'm sure that you have, but I have never had any advance notification that the test was just around the corner. That's why I am absolutely convinced that all of the tests in the Christian life are pop quizzes. You never know *when* your faith will be tested, and you never know *how* your faith will be tested.

What will God test in these pop quizzes? He will definitely test our faith. At other times, He may test our obedience. Every now and then, He will test our integrity. God will test our ability to trust and He will test our willingness to stand alone. He will test our character from numerous different angles in order to assure that genuine maturity is actually taking hold in our lives. Why? Because He is conforming us into the image of Christ.

Since pop quizzes are such a normal part of the Christian life, let's look at these unique tests a little more closely.

POP QUIZZES ARE SURPRISING

Beloved, do not be *surprised* at the fiery ordeal among you, which comes upon you for your testing, as though some strange thing were happening to you. (1 Peter 4:12, emphasis added)

Let's face it. You and I are usually surprised when the furnace heats up. I don't know about you, but for the longest time, suffering always took me by surprise—just like a pop quiz. I never took a pop quiz without being surprised and I have never suffered without being surprised.

I think there are two reasons why we are so consistently surprised.

REASON #1: OVERSELL EVANGELISM

"Are you having difficulties in your life? Is your life falling apart? Are there insurmountable hardships that are threatening to overwhelm you? Then give your life to Christ. Jesus Christ will take away all of those things and give you a brand-new life."

Have you ever heard an evangelistic appeal similar to that? I certainly have. The only problem with it is this: It isn't true. Sometimes, in our zeal to see people come to Jesus Christ, we oversell the gospel. How do we do that? Simple. In our enthusiasm to persuade someone to make a "decision" for Christ, we make promises to them that Jesus Christ never made.

The truth is, Jesus never promised to take away our troubles, our hardships, or our sufferings. On the contrary, He clearly told us that we would encounter precisely these things simply because we belong to Him!

Do you remember when Jesus told His disciples that in the world they would have an easy time? You probably don't, because He never said it. Jesus said, "In the world you have tribulation" (John 16:33).

Paul wrote to the Philippian church and declared, "For to you it has been granted for Christ's sake, not only to believe in Him, but also to suffer for His sake" (Philippians 1:29).

The fact of the matter is that neither Jesus Christ nor His Word ever promised that our troubles and hardships would be taken away. Jesus promised to take away our sins, not our hardships. If you came to Christ after hearing some deficient promises, then it's little wonder you were surprised the first time you were tested.

The gospel is the power of God unto salvation. It is neither wise nor necessary to add additional promises to the gospel. God does not need us to edit the gospel with promises of a trouble-free Christian life.

REASON #2: BABY BOOMER EXPECTATIONS

If you were born between 1946 and 1964, then you are a card-carrying member of the Baby Boomer generation. What in the world does that have to do with being surprised by testing?

Landon Jones tells us that the baby boom generation is:

> ...above all the biggest, richest, and best-educated generation America ever produced. The boom babies were born to be the best and the brightest. Blessed with the great expectations of affluence and education, the boom children were raised as the generation of idealism and hope....
>
> Unlike their parents and grandparents who scrimped, saved, and struggled through the Depression and World War II eras, the early baby boomers were told that they could have it all. Non-stop advertising promised instant gratification that could be had now and paid for later. [3]

As Mike Bellah has observed, "Never in the history of our country has a generation been taught to expect more from life. Never has a generation been more disappointed and disillusioned as adults." Doug Murren concurs when he comments that "we baby boomers are possibly the most spoiled generation ever to come along."[4]

Now maybe you're a baby boomer, and you're sitting there thinking that you're not so sure that you were brought up in affluence or that you were spoiled. Your family was just basic middle class. But stop and think about it. Compared to any other generation in the history of civilization, we baby boomers had more affluence and ease than any who have ever walked the earth. Your family may have been middle class, but just about anyone else in the history of the world would look at you and say that you lived like kings.

Our parents came back from World War II and were able to buy their own homes, thanks to special financing provided for veterans. The option of college was open to many for the first time through the GI Bill. Then Jonas Salk discovered the polio vaccine, and as a result, we were free from the fear of polio, which both literally and figuratively paralyzed our parents' generation.

It is no exaggeration to say that we baby boomers had an easy life. We had it easy when it came to affluence and health. So it's not really surprising that we were stunned the very first time we hit a few rapids on the smooth, lazy river of our lives. If life has basically been a sleepy glide along the Swanee River, then there will inevitably be some surprise when we hit Class IV white-water rapids that test us for the very first time.

POP QUIZZES ARE INEVITABLE

Consider it all joy, my brethren, *when* you encounter various trials.... (James 1:2, emphasis added)

Please notice that James did not say *if* you encounter various trials, he said *when*. The trials that comprise the hardships of our various pop quizzes are not optional; they are inevitable.

It was F. B. Meyer who said, "If I'm told that I'm in for a hard journey, every hard jolt along the way reminds me that I'm on the right road."

Contrary to the superficial teaching of some, the abundant life is not a life characterized by the absence of hardship. Every time you get a jolt or a shock from the circumstances of your life, it is a stiff reminder that you are on the right road. That's why endurance is so important in the Christian life. It takes endurance to remain faithful when the potholes of life threaten to swallow us alive.

D. Martyn Lloyd-Jones wrote of these hard times:

> These things happen…because they are good for us, because they are a part of our discipline in this life and in this world, because—let me put it quite plainly—because God has appointed it .
>
> There is a very definite plan and purpose of the whole of my life, God has looked upon me, God has adopted me and put me into His family. What for? In order that He may bring me to perfection (maturity)…. The doctrine of the Scriptures is, at the very lowest, that God permits these things to happen to us. I go further, God at times orders these things to happen to us for our good.[5]

There's an old line that only two things in life are inevitable: death and taxes. But that's not quite accurate. I lived most of my life in California, and as a result, I have been in numerous earthquakes. When I was four, I was in the biggest earthquake in the history of California. I can still remember driving around town the next day with my grandfather and seeing the devastation. When you live in California, earthquakes are inevitable.

Now we live in Texas and I don't think much about earthquakes. But several blocks from our house is a very large tower. I wasn't sure what it was at first, but now I know it's a tornado siren. When you live in Texas, tornadoes are inevitable.

The story is told of a man who for years had walked the high steel girders of giant skyscrapers under construction in New York. Danger is an inevitable part of working on girders suspended hundreds of feet in the air. One late afternoon, just before quitting time, a difficulty arose with a crane, and as the foreman he had to stay until the problem was solved. It was now dark, and as he gingerly made his way to the exit he suddenly tripped and lost his balance. As he fell through the darkness, he managed to reach out and grab the edge of a girder. He clung desperately, hoping that someone would hear his calls for help. But no one heard.

It was dark, he was alone, and the frantic sounds of the rushing city drowned out his cries. Gradually his arms grew numb. He held on for as long as he could muster the strength. One by one his fingers gave way, and finally he could hold his weight no more. Into the darkness he fell with a terrified scream. His body landed on a scaffold—ten inches below—that had been there all the time.

It's true that pop quizzes are inevitable, but that's okay. There's plenty of scaffolding to go around.

POP QUIZZES ARE DIVERSE

Consider it all joy, my brethren, when you encounter *various* trials…. (James 1:2, emphasis added)

Henry Ford used to say that you could buy the Model T in any color you wanted…as long as it was black. Today, cars come in a multitude of colors. So do trials. The Greek word here translated *various* actually carries the idea of *many colored*. [6] "The term is comprehensive. It means anything in this life that tends to trouble you, something that touches you in the most sensitive and delicate part of your being, in your heart, in your mind, the things that tend to cast you down."[7]

In other words, we will all be tested, but the tests will be different. God allows different situations in the lives of different people. That's why the testing that comes your way will be different than the testing your best friend encounters.

This explains why comparison is such a dangerous habit. When we are being tested, we look around at our friends and see that none of them are dealing with the same, hard issues that seem to be plaguing us. Let's say, for instance, that you are unable to have children. You've been through all the tests and seen all the specialists, but to no avail. As a result, it may be difficult for you to understand why all of your friends have no problem at all conceiving babies. Some of them are so fertile that they can seemingly get pregnant by just standing in the same room. But not you. Those other couples, however, are dealing with completely different tests than you are.

They may be dealing with a financial reversal, a handicapped child, a malignant tumor, or a reputation in the process of being shredded by a vicious rumor. From our perspective it looks as though we are the only ones being tested. But nothing could be further from the truth.

As J. I. Packer has noted, suffering is getting what you do not want while wanting what you do not get. And that's why comparison is such a deadly indoor sport.

POP QUIZZES ARE PURPOSEFUL

Everyone suffers. But Christians suffer on purpose. Or, to be more accurate, Christians suffer *with* a purpose. As James put it, "Knowing that the testing of your faith produces endurance" (1:3). Paul amplifies that thought when he writes:

> And not only this, but we also exult in our tribulations, knowing that tribulation brings about perseverance; and perseverance, proven character; and proven character, hope; and hope does not disappoint...." (Romans 5:3–5)

"What is God's purpose in trials?" asks Warren Wiersbe. "It is the perfection of Christian character in His children. He wants his children to be mature, and maturity is developed only in the laboratory of life."[8]

Tests and trials always go hand in hand and for the believer they have a definite purpose. Elisabeth Elliot has observed that "in God's management of the affairs of men, suffering is never senseless." God never allows us to suffer randomly—His hand is in the testing and on the testing, making sure that His purpose is accomplished. God always has a specific goal in mind when He allows us to encounter a pop quiz. There is something in particular that He wants to test. Consider the multiple pop quizzes sprung upon the following individual:

> When he was seven years old, his family was forced out of their home on a legal technicality, and he had to work to help support them.

At age nine, his mother died.

At twenty-two, he lost his job as a store clerk. He wanted to go to law school, but his education wasn't good enough.

At twenty-three, he went into debt to become a partner in a small store.

At twenty-six, his business partner died, leaving him a huge debt that took years to repay.

At twenty-eight, after courting a girl for four years, he asked her to marry him. She said no.

At thirty-seven, on his third try, he was elected to Congress, but two years later he failed to be reelected.

At forty-one, his four-year-old son died.

At forty-five, he ran for the Senate and lost.

At forty-seven, he failed as the vice presidential candidate.

At forty-nine, he ran again for the Senate and lost.

At fifty-one, he was elected president of the United States.

His name was Abraham Lincoln, a man many consider the greatest leader the country ever had. Some people get all the breaks.[9]

When God created Abraham Lincoln, He had a great work for him to do. No wonder Lincoln had so many tests. That's why he endured the heat of the furnace—so that the steel in his soul might be tempered and strong.

During his first presidential debates, Bill Clinton said in essence that *personal* character is not the issue. The issue is the character of the presidency." He could not have been more wrong. Lincoln was a great president because he had great character. Lincoln's character was tested and developed through the fiery disappointments of life. And Lincoln passed every test. Great character is the cumulative result when great pain and great disappointment intersect in a man with a teachable spirit.

God was looking for a man for an impossible task, so He purposed to take Abraham Lincoln through the tests of life to qualify him for the ceaseless strain that the job would require. Abraham Lincoln was tested for a purpose. And so are we.

Lincoln was born in 1809. George Mueller was born in 1805. Mueller is best known for his orphanages in England that brought care and salvation to numerous orphans, beginning in 1835. Mueller, who was usually penniless, trusted God completely to meet the large financial burdens of caring for so many children. Although he died in 1895, Mueller is still remembered as a man of great faith. It was Mueller who wrote that "God delights to increase the faith of His children. We ought, instead of wanting no trials before victory, no exercise for patience, to be willing to take them from God's hand as a means. I say—and say it deliberately—trials, obstacles, difficulties, and sometimes defeats, are the very food of faith."[10]

Mueller lived out what he preached. In 1870, after thirty-nine years of marriage, Mueller's wife, Mary, died of rheumatic fever. They had been exceptionally close, and it was a deep and devastating blow to Mueller. Yet it was Mueller who spoke at his wife's funeral. His text was Psalm 119:68, "You are good, and do good." Mueller made three observations from the psalm:

1. The Lord was good, and did good, in giving her to me.
2. The Lord was good, and did good, in so long leaving her to me.
3. The Lord was good, and did good, in taking her from me.[11]

George Mueller, even in the grief of his loss, had a faith that was remarkably strong. That faith was not the result of a life of ease and affluence. It was the result of test after test. Yet George Mueller knew God and he had the maturity to trust in the goodness of God's character. As Oswald Chambers once said, "You rarely hear a man who has been through the real agony of suffering who says he disbelieves in God, it is the one who watches others going through suffering who says he disbelieves in God." That was true in Mueller's life, and it was true in Lincoln's.

The character of these two men was deeply tested. They all drank deeply from the well of disappointment and defeat. Both of these men are dead. Yet their character lives on to this day as an example to countless others. Why? The answer is simple. Their character was proven. Their character was tested, deeply tested, by the pop quizzes of a loving Father. They passed the test, and their character is the untarnished trophy that continues to live on to this day.

The Football Hall of Fame is in Canton, Ohio. The Basketball Hall of Fame is in Springfield, Massachusetts. The Baseball Hall of Fame is in Cooperstown, New York. I can't prove this, but I believe that there is a Character Hall of Fame. It's in heaven. Unless I miss my guess, George Mueller and Abraham Lincoln are both in it. And they've got the scars to prove it.

Pop Quizzes are BRIEF

Does this one surprise you? Pop quizzes in school are almost always very short in duration, but the tests of the Christian life seem at times to be the exact opposite! When I think about the tests I have been through, the very last word that comes to mind is *brief*. Yet note the words of Peter:

> In this you greatly rejoice, even though now for a *little while,* if necessary, you have been distressed by various trials, so that the proof of your faith, being more precious than gold which is perishable, even though tested by fire, may be found to result in praise and glory and honor at the revelation of Jesus Christ. (1 Peter 1:6–7, emphasis added)

Time is a matter of perspective. When I was a child, I was convinced that Christmas came every two or three years. It was such a long time between Christmases, and the last week before Christmas seemed to somehow slow down time so that it actually expanded into six months. Waiting for Christmas was a very slow process that made every day seem like it was in slow motion. Now that I'm a parent, I'm convinced that Christmas comes every six months!

It's really a matter of perspective, isn't it?

When you are in the middle of a pop quiz and your faith is being tested by some type of adversity, it can seem like it will go on forever. But it won't. It just feels that way.

The King James Version translates "a little while" as "for a season." I like that. Seasons come and go. Just when you think that the hot and humid days will never end, you wake up one morning, go outside to get the paper, and you are greeted by the first cool day of fall. There's a nip in the air, and you know that summer is over and fall is on the way. We suffer for a season, for a little while. That's the nature of God's pop quizzes. Martyn Lloyd-Jones describes it with magnificence and hope:

> Do not get the impression that I am teaching that this state of trial is the perpetual state of the Christian. It is not. These things come and go as God deems fit. We shall never be tried and tested except it be for our good, and as we respond to the teaching, God will withdraw the test. He does not keep us permanently under trial.
>
> He is your loving Father, He knows how much you can take and stand. He will never send too much for you. He knows the right amount, and He will give the right amount, and when you have responded He will withdraw it. It is only "for a season." Do these words come to some downcast, heavy-laden Christian? Does all seem blackness and darkness? Are you not having the liberty you once had in prayer? Have you almost lost the faith you once had? Do not be troubled. You are in the hand of your Father. There may be a glorious period coming for you, He may have some great work for you to do. Do not be downcast. It is only "for a season." You are in the hands of your loving Father, so trust Him and go on.[12]

Climbing the Character Ladder

It doesn't take but a short time on the educational ladder before a first grader realizes that testing is a normal part of life in school. After three or four weeks, he's starting to get the hang of how life works in first grade. By the time a first grader is on Christmas vacation, he has already experienced a full menu of tests: arithmetic tests, spelling tests, geography tests, etc. As a result, very young children are no longer surprised when they encounter a test. They have come to realize that tests are a normal and expected part of climbing the educational ladder.

Every Christian, whether he realizes it or not, has a heavenly Father who also has a ladder for His children to climb. But it's not the same ladder we spoke of earlier. *The primary ladder in the life of a believer is the character lad-*

der. Just as we ascended the educational ladder through various stages of schooling designed to increase our knowledge, so God has a character ladder that He wants us to ascend so that our character might be conformed into the image of Jesus Christ.

God has a goal for me, and He has a goal for you. He wants to conform us to the image of Jesus Christ (Romans 8:29). I don't know about you, but as far as I'm concerned, that is going to require massive change.

The average five-year-old child might be able to spell a few words and add one plus one. Some can and some can't. Generally speaking, five-year-olds can't read, can't do math, can't understand quantum physics, can't design computer software, and can't understand the federal tax code. But the reason that we have children climb the educational ladder over a long period of time is so that they might eventually be educated to the point where they have the knowledge, skill, and expertise to do any or all of those tasks (except understand the tax code).

In other words, parents have very high goals for their five-year-olds. The goal of the educational ladder is to take a valuable person who is illiterate and uneducated and transform him into someone who is literate and educated.

Our heavenly Father wants to see us grow and develop as well. He does not desire for me to stay in spiritual kindergarten. He wants to see me realize my potential in Christ. That's why it is His desire that I climb the character ladder, for the higher I climb on the character ladder, the more I become conformed to the image of Jesus Christ.

Should we ever be surprised then that testing is such a major part of the Christian life? There are no shortcuts to spiritual maturity. I cannot continue to mature in Christ without my faith being tested.

That's why pop quizzes are such a normal part of the Christian life. That's why my faith is tested and your faith is tested. That's why some of you reading these words are in tremendous pain and turmoil. God is at work! From your perspective it may seem that things have never been this bad before in your life. Where is God in all of this? Has He forgotten all about you? Has He abandoned you? It may certainly seem that way in the middle of an arduous test. But there's another perspective, and John Piper states it well:

When things are going "bad," that does not mean that God has stopped doing good. It means that He is shifting things around to get them in place for more good, if you will go on loving Him.[13]

Chiseled in Stone

Mount Rushmore is one of the most stupendous pieces of human work in the world. It is the artistry of the great sculptor, Gutzon Borglum. Many believe, however, that the greatest work Mr. Borglum ever did was the head of Lincoln in the capitol at Washington. Borglum cut it from a block of marble that had long been in his private studio at home.

It is said that an old black woman, a former slave, would often clean that studio for Mr. Borglum, along with the rest of the house. She was very familiar with the block of marble that had been in the studio for the longest time. One morning she came in and saw to her astonishment and terror the unmistakable lines of Lincoln appearing in the stone. She ran to Borglum's secretary and said, "Is that Abraham Lincoln?"

"Yes," replied the secretary, "that's Mr. Lincoln."

With great awe she inquired, "How in the world did Mr. Borglum know that Mr. Lincoln was in that stone?"[14]

God looked at Abraham Lincoln and knew that He wanted to sculpt a man of tested character. So He took him through many pop quizzes, those difficult, sudden, and unannounced tests that come from the hand of God. And as time went on, the lines of Jesus Christ became more and more apparent in the character of Lincoln.

That's precisely what testing is designed to do.

It was the process that God used in Lincoln's life.

It was the process that God used in David's life.

So are you in the pit of testing as you read these pages? Are you in the deepest and most difficult test of your entire life? Are you beginning to wonder if God has forgotten about you? Are you starting to think He doesn't care about you? Those are the telltale signs that you are indeed being tested.

But here is the truth of the matter.

He hasn't forgotten about you. He knows how bad you are hurting, and yes, He does care. But He also sees what you can't see at the specific moment.

He sees what He wants you to become. He sees the day when He will bring you out of the pit. He knows the day when this test will be over. You don't.

Lincoln couldn't see what God had in store for him.

Neither could David.

Both men had their days when they wondered if they would actually *get through* the tests. But we're still talking about both men years and years after they finished the trail.

We are talking about them *because* they were tested. And if that's where you find yourself today, be encouraged.

You're in good company.

He got them through.

He will get you through.

FOR SUCH A TIME AS THIS...

America is facing days of crisis unlike any we have experienced since the days of Lincoln. And the question has been, where would we ever find the kind of giant oak from which such a giant beam could be fashioned and hewn?

God always has a stand of oaks that are obscure and away from the view of most everyone except him. He plants them and cultivates them centuries before they are needed. But at the right time, He brings them into service. They have been tested and will be tested.

"Great crises bring forth great leaders," wrote Abigail Adams. And it is God who designs and oversees both.

All of God's men are tested. But in every century there are a handful who are placed on the stage of world events when civilization is at stake. We are in such a crisis now. Years ago, a businessman addressed an audience at the Teen Challenge Center in Lubbock, Texas. In his speech he made this statement:

"I was an alcoholic and Jesus saved me not only from alcoholism, but from sin. I've given my heart to Jesus Christ."[15]

George W. Bush has been through some tough tests. But he is facing one right now that only a few men face in the course of a century. Just several years ago, he was a relatively obscure Texas businessman who was making some decisions for a baseball team. Now he's making decisions that will affect the course of human history.

That's a test I wouldn't want to take. But he has been raised up for such a time as this. And the test before us is to pray for him.

So how do we pray for him?

I would suggest we pray that he becomes a Josiah instead of an Amaziah. Josiah and Amaziah were two kings of Judah. It was said of Amaziah that "he did right in the sight of the LORD, yet not with a whole heart" (2 Chronicles 25:2).

King Josiah was the greatest king of the Old Testament. Even greater than David. Why? "And he did right in the sight of the LORD and walked in all the way of his father David, nor did he turn aside to the right or to the left" (2 Kings 22:2). Josiah never got sidetracked with major sin, as David did. The following statement that God recorded about Josiah nails down his position as the greatest of all the kings of Israel and Judah:

> Before him there was no king like him who turned to the LORD with all his heart and with all his soul and with all his might, according to all the law of Moses; nor did any like him arise after him. (2 Kings 23:25)

Just seven days after the September 11 attack, George Bush appointed Michael E. Guest as the United States ambassador to Romania. Guest is an avowed homosexual. During the swearing-in ceremony for Guest, Secretary of State Colin Powell acknowledged Guest's "domestic partner" who will live in the embassy with him. So now we have a homosexual ambassador living in the American embassy with his homosexual lover. That is beyond belief.

I didn't expect that from George W. Bush. He's a better man than that. A much better man.

President Bush has a decision to make. He must decide if he will be an Amaziah or a Josiah. He must decide if he will listen to liberal advisors or the Word of God. It took Bill Clinton seven years to appoint homosexual James Hormel as an ambassador to Luxembourg. It took George Bush just seven months to do the same. God will not bless America and He will not bless President Bush if those kinds of appointments continue to be made.

The task in front of George Bush is to decide if he will be an Amaziah or a Josiah when it comes to standing up against perversion.

Our task is to diligently pray that he will pass the test. We thank God for a president, who according to his father, has read the Bible through—cover to cover—twice. Now we need to pray that he will implement all that is in that Bible. And, while we're at it, let's pray for ourselves that we will do the same thing. That's always the ultimate test.

THREE

ROBINSON CRUSOE

*I was now entered on the seven and twentieth year of my captivity
in this place...with the same thankfulness to God
for his mercies as at the first....*

ROBINSON CRUSOE

A FEW MONTHS AGO, I SAW THE MOVIE *CAST AWAY*, starring Tom Hanks. It was
something of a modernized Robinson Crusoe story, with Hanks playing the
part of a FedEx executive riding a large cargo jet across the ocean. When the
jet crashes into the sea, Hanks' character is the only survivor. He is swept up
by the waves onto a remote island, hundred of miles away from the shipping
lanes. For years, the luckless executive has to learn to fend for himself and
survive.

I really didn't like this movie. And I'll tell you why.

Here's a guy who has lost *everything*, with little hope of ever being found.
It's the greatest, most daunting challenge he has ever faced in his lifetime.
And do you suppose that the thought of God or prayer ever crosses this des-
perate man's mind?

Not even once.

It's as though the idea of praying, the instinctive reaction of human
beings since the dawn of time, is as strange and foreign as a driver's manual
from Mars.

Distressed and needy as he is, the thought of calling out to God is utterly
alien to him. Why would he need God? He draws a face on a Wilson vol-
leyball and makes believe he's found a companion and friend. God is

nowhere on the scene, and even in his darkest hour, the castaway doesn't need Him.

Here's a guy who had it made, and *bam! whoosh!* A trapdoor suddenly opens beneath his feet, dropping him into the biggest, deepest pit of his life. No problem! He can handle everything just fine.

That, my friends, is the deceptive message of our culture.

After watching *Cast Away,* the next afternoon I took a little drive to our local bookstore and bought a copy of *Robinson Crusoe* by Daniel Defoe. I hadn't read that book since high school. (In fact, I'm not even sure I read it then. I think I remember skimming through the CliffsNotes.)

Now why did I pick up *Robinson Crusoe*? For two reasons. First, I knew enough about the book to figure out that *Cast Away* was a modern-day rip-off of the story Defoe had written over 250 years ago. I wanted to read the original story for myself. Second, I remembered reading an old sermon by Charles Haddon Spurgeon, which he had preached in the 1880s. In that sermon, the great preacher referenced Psalm 50:14–15. Spurgeon called that psalm "the Robinson Crusoe psalm" and mentioned that that particular passage was Robinson Crusoe's favorite. Here's what it says:

> Offer to God a sacrifice of thanksgiving
> And pay your vows to the Most High;
> Call upon Me in the day of trouble;
> I shall rescue you, and you will honor Me.

That was enough to make me curious about Robinson Crusoe. I had to check this guy out.

HERE'S TO YOU, MR. ROBINSON

Over the next few days, I read the entire story of Robinson Crusoe. Not only is it one of the best novels I've ever read, it's one of the best Christian books I've ever read. The truth of the Bible is everywhere in that book.

That probably explains why you won't find it on the reading lists of high school English classes these days; there's just too much Christianity in those pages. Defoe's novel, completed in 1719, became wildly popular in England.

It was a riveting adventure, but it also pointed people to the one they could call on when they found themselves in the pit.

Allow me to give you a quick flyover of the Robinson Crusoe story. In essence, this young man was the prodigal son. While still a lad living at home, Robinson had several serious talks with his father. The elder Crusoe gave his son sound advice about his conduct and about his future. But young Robinson would hear nothing of it. He wanted to go to sea and make his fortune—even though his father warned him again and again about the hardships of such a life.

One day Robinson was at the docks in his hometown of York. On impulse, he signed on with a ship and left without leaving word for his parents. On this, his first voyage, a storm immediately came up, and the young runaway became deathly sick. In his heart, he knew that God was reprimanding him for his disobedience. The other sailors laughed at him because it was such a minor storm, but to Robinson, it was the worst calamity of his life. He vowed that if God would get him to port safely, he would return to his father and never sail again.

Shortly thereafter, the storm ceased. For the next week the weather was perfect, the sea was calm, and Robinson quickly forgot his vows. During this peaceful interlude, he got into a drinking contest with some of his shipmates.

But then another storm hit.

This storm went on for days, and when Robinson overheard the captain crying out to God to save them, he knew they were in desperate straits. The ship went down, but another ship was able to rescue the crew. Upon arriving on shore, the ship's owner told young Robinson that "the hand of Providence" was instructing him not to go to sea. He should return to his father's house. The older man warned him that if he did not do so, disaster would follow him for the rest of his life.

Robinson ignored the warning, taking some of his money and investing it in yet another voyage. He was very successful. But on the voyage after that, he was captured by pirates and taken as a slave. He managed to escape and make his way to Brazil. In doing so, he killed a leopard and a massive lion with his rifle and, with the help of another escaped slave, skinned both animals. Later he sold the skins and a small boat for a great profit, which enabled him to buy a plantation in Brazil.

Now that he had accumulated some wealth, he wanted more. He agreed to finance another voyage, this time planning to buy slaves and sell them.

It was during this voyage that his ship encountered another violent storm. Everyone was killed except Robinson Crusoe. Swept up on the shore of a deserted island, he immediately did something that Tom Hank's character never did.

He praised God for His mercy and grace in saving him from the storm.

Robinson Crusoe had been on the verge of becoming a reprobate. But he had enough sense to realize that he had not saved himself. Kneeling there on that lonely beach, he offered to God a sacrifice of praise for sparing his life. He would call that remote and lifeless island home for the next twenty-seven years of his life.

That island became his own personal Engedi.

BACK TO DAVID

En-what?

Engedi.

Sort of sounds like a new SUV, doesn't it? Expedition, Suburban, Yukon, Dakota, Denali, Escalade, Engedi.

But Engedi isn't an SUV. Engedi is a place. A lonely, empty place where David, the psalmist, poured out his heart to the Lord.

In the last chapter, we left David running for his life from Saul. When the trapdoor opened under that young man's feet and the bottom fell out from under his life, one of the places David landed was Engedi. When David realized that Saul was insanely committed to killing him, he took to the hills—specifically, the hills that ran down from Jerusalem to the arid, hot desert surrounding the Dead Sea. Remember, Saul was king of Israel and had his army and his intelligence network looking for David twenty-four hours a day, seven days a week. And this went on for years.

Engedi is an oasis. It's in the middle of the Judean desert, just to the west of the Dead Sea. The temperature in that desert can get close to 120. I know, because I've been there in the middle of July. Maybe that's why Engedi is my favorite place in all of Israel. When you're climbing the trails of Engedi, it's a historical certainty that you are walking the same trails that David walked three thousand years ago.

Engedi is in the middle of nowhere, surrounded by mile after mile of even more nowhere. It is a barren, empty, windswept desert—a dead land, next to the Dead Sea. But just west of the Dead Sea, nestled up against the hills, is the oasis called Engedi.

As you turn west from the Dead Sea into the ravine between the hills, you suddenly come upon a clear, running stream of cold water. You can hardly believe your eyes. Hike a few minutes up the hill and you'll encounter a beautiful pool surrounded by large boulders and fed by a waterfall that drops from sixty or seventy feet above. Not only is there cold, refreshing water, but there are lush, majestic palms full of dates, and magnificent vine-yards further on up the hill.

The first thing you notice as you climb up this ravine is how narrow it is—probably only a hundred feet at its widest. As you glance up at the walls of that canyon, you can see numerous caves and huge, fern-like bushes that grow lush and thick to nearly ten feet tall.

The last time I hiked up that stream toward the waterfall, I stopped for a rest next to one of those mammoth ferns. It crossed my mind that David, or one of his men, could hide behind those things and you wouldn't be able to see them from two feet away. And that's exactly what David did. He hid in the caves and flora, coming and going for years. In this way, and in this place, David escaped Saul's dragnet.

David wrote Psalm 57 as he was hiding from Saul in that honeycomb of caves at Engedi. In many Bibles, you will see that fact written right into the descriptive wording right below the chapter heading.

This is a "cave" psalm. A psalm from the pit. David is literally hiding out when he's writing it!

Be gracious to me, O God, be gracious to me,
For my soul takes refuge in You;
And in the shadow of Your wings I will take refuge
Until destruction passes by.
I will cry to God Most High,

To God who accomplishes all things for me.
He will send from heaven and save me;
He reproaches him who tramples upon me. Selah.
God will send forth His lovingkindness and His truth.
My soul is among lions;
I must lie among those who breathe forth fire,
Even the sons of men, whose teeth are spears and arrows
And their tongue a sharp sword.
Be exalted above the heavens, O God;
Let Your glory be above all the earth.
They have prepared a net for my steps;
My soul is bowed down;
They dug a pit before me;
They themselves have fallen into the midst of it. Selah.
My heart is steadfast, O God, my heart is steadfast;
I will sing, yes, I will sing praises!
Awake, my glory!
Awake, harp and lyre!
I will awaken the dawn.
I will give thanks to You, O Lord, among the peoples;
I will sing praises to You among the nations.
For Your lovingkindness is great to the heavens
And Your truth to the clouds.
Be exalted above the heavens, O God;
Let Your glory be above all the earth. (emphasis added)

Did you catch the phrase in that second verse? "To God who accomplishes all things for me." Let's chew on that phrase a moment or two. Within those words, I believe we will discover the secret of David's survival through those long, fugitive years. And it will be the same secret that Robinson Crusoe discovered on that lonely island.

David was in extreme danger, and so was Robinson Crusoe. When David uttered these words, everything was against him. No one would have given David a snowball's chance in hades of escaping.

But David cried unto God the Most High. Yes, King Saul was dead set against David, and Saul was the highest man in all of Israel. But David goes over Saul's head to the Most High. He calls to the God "who accomplishes (or performs) all things for me."

This word *accomplish* comes from a root that signifies accomplishing work and then ceasing or desisting from that work.[1] Psalm 138:8 states "the LORD will accomplish what concerns me." David knew that he was a work in progress. He knew that God had promised him the throne of Israel. That work would be accomplished by God. God would fulfill His promise to David. Therefore, David knew that he wouldn't die. The work that God promised to do had not yet been accomplished. As someone has well said, "The servant of the Lord is indestructible until God is finished with him."

David didn't know how it would all work out, but he knew that the invisible hand of Providence would bring God's plan for his life to completion.

This is really the sense of Psalm 57:2. In fact, some scholars have rendered it in the following ways to pick up the sense of the root ideas:

I will cry unto God most high, unto God that performeth the things which he hath promised.[2]
I will cry unto God the Most High, the transactor of my affairs.[3]

This is the thought that allowed David to give praise to God in the midst of being chased by Saul's henchmen. David was able to trust God when he was on the run, because he held on to the promise that he would one day sit on the throne.

The truth is, God oversees all of the personal affairs of his people. John Flavel gives us more flavoring on the providence of God, and how it works in our lives. And remember, this includes the unscheduled pit stops.

His providence not only has its hand in this or that, but in all that concerns them (believers). It has its eye upon everything that relates to them throughout their lives, from first to last. Not only the great and more important, but the most minute and ordinary affairs of our lives are transacted and managed by it; it touches all things that touch us...nearly or remotely.

It goes through with its designs, and accomplishes what it begins. No difficulty so clogs it, no cross accidents fall in its way, but it carries its design through it. Its motions are irresistible and uncontrollable; He performs it for us.[4]

Bing Hunter states in more contemporary terms:

Because of God's providential care for his creation, ultimately, there is no such thing as luck. What is more, from God's perspective, there are not really any accidents, surprises, or "curious turns of history." What we call chance doesn't exist. Sound extreme? Yes it does. But these ideas are straightforward consequences of verses like Proverbs 16:33: "The lot is cast into the lap, but its every decision is from the LORD." From a biblical perspective, your world-history book should be prefaced with 2 Kings 19:25, "Have you not heard. Long ago I ordained it. In the days of old I planned it; now I have brought it to pass."[5]

No matter where you are in life, no matter how dark your present circumstances, you can stand on the providence of God. Sometimes it may seem as though providence has quit working for you. But it hasn't. Thomas Watson reminds us that God is at work even when we don't see any evidence of His work.

God is to be trusted when his providences seem to run contrary to His promises. God promised David to give him the crown to make him king; but providence turns contrary to His promise. David was pursued by Saul and in danger of his life; but in all this it was David's duty to trust God. The Lord, does often, by cross providences, bring to pass His promise. God promised Paul the lives of all that were with him in the ship; but now the providence of God seems to run quite contrary to His promise; the wind blows, the ship splits and breaks in pieces; and thus God fulfilled His promise; upon the broken pieces of the ship, they all come safe to the shore. Trust God when providences seem to run quite contrary to promises.[6]

That's a very unique twist to the normal way of looking at life in the pit. But God is the transactor of all of my affairs. *All of them.* Even when I find myself in the pit. It was this type of thinking that completely changed Robinson Crusoe—even though his circumstances didn't change one whit.

Robinson Crusoe was a prodigal son. He was an unbeliever who had rejected the good, biblical counsel of his father. He was running full speed away from God and headed for destruction. So God stepped in and put him in the pit. Maybe that rings a bell with you. Like Crusoe, if you are running against God, you are in a losing effort. God will hem you in and exhaust you and reduce you to nothing if He so wills to get your attention. Yes, you can make disobedient and foolish decisions that will cost you. You can create your own hell on earth. But God is always bigger than we are. Out of His mercy, He can pull a trapdoor and put us in the pit to turn our hearts to Him.

God pulled the chain on Robinson Crusoe, and he found himself on a deserted island. But it was all for his ultimate good. And within days of landing on the island, Crusoe actually began to see the first rays of God's goodness. He sat down with his pen, ink, and paper, which he had salvaged from the ship along with a number of other items, and made a ledger. Not a ledger of accounts, but a ledger of the bad and good in his life. He actually divided the page in half and wrote "Evil" on one side and "Good" on the other.

Robinson Crusoe was in the pit, but he began to do something on a daily basis that is good advice for anyone in some kind of pit. He began to write down his thoughts:

I now began to consider seriously my condition, and the circumstance I was reduced to; and I drew up the state of my affairs in writing, not so much to leave them to any that were to come after me (for I was like to have but few heirs), as to deliver my thoughts from daily poring upon them, and afflicting my mind: and as my reason began no to master my despondency, I began to comfort myself as well as I could, and to set the good against the evil, that I might have something to distinguish my case from the worse; and I stated very impartially, like debtor and creditor, the comforts I enjoyed against the miseries I suffered, thus:

EVIL	GOOD
I am cast upon a horrible, desolate island, void of all hope of recovery.	But I am alive; and not drowned, as all my ship's company were
I am singled out and separated, as it were, from all the world, to be miserable.	But I am singled out from all the ship's crew to be spared from death; and He that miraculously saved me from death, can deliver me from this condition.
I am divided from mankind, a solitaire; one banished from human society. I have no clothes to cover me.	But I am not starved, and perishing in a barren place, affording no sustenance. But I am in a hot climate where if I had clothes I could hardly wear them.
I am without any defense, or means to resist any violence of man or beast.	But I am on an island where I see no wild beasts to hurt me, as I saw on the coast of Africa; and what if I had been ship-wrecked there?
I have no soul to speak to, or relieve me.	But God wonderfully sent the ship in near enough to the shore, that I have got out so many necessary things, as will either supply my wants, or enable me to supply myself, even as long as I live.

Upon the whole, here was an unbounded testimony, that there was scarce any condition in the world so miserable, but there was something negative, or something positive, to be thankful for in it; and let this stand as a direction, from the experience of the most miserable of all conditions in this world, that we may always find in it something to comfort ourselves from, and to set, in the description of good and evil, on the credit side of the account.[7]

What Robinson Crusoe is saying is this: Hidden in every desert is an oasis; hidden in every pit is an Engedi.

May I offer a suggestion to you? If you are struggling with a particular set of circumstances, why don't you take the first opportunity you can find to get in a quiet place, take a piece of paper and a pen, and do what Robinson Crusoe did.

Take that paper and draw a line in the middle from top to bottom. Now you've got two columns. Write "evil" on the left side, and "good" on the right. Start listing the bad stuff—but don't stop there. Go over to the right side of the paper and write out the good as well. As you do the same exercise that Robinson Crusoe did, you will discover that as bad as that pit may be, it's not *all* bad.

God has provided an oasis in your desert.

Somewhere in your pit is an Engedi.

BAD DREAMS

A few days later, Robinson became violently ill. While he was in that condition, he had a horrible dream that sickened him emotionally. In his diary for June 28 he recounts that this was a day when he first began to feel better. He was still extremely weak, but he managed to put together a small meal. And then he recorded something remarkable: For the first time in his adult life, he bowed his head and thanked God for the provision of food he was about to enjoy. After his meal he staggered out a ways from his camp, where he sat down and looked out at the sea. As you read his reflections, note how logical and clear his thinking is:

As I sat here, some such thoughts as these occurred to me: What is the earth and the sea, of which I have seen so much? Whence is it produced? And what am I, and all the other creatures, wild and tame, human and brutal? Whence are we? Surely, we are all made by some secret power, who formed the earth and sea, the air and sky. And who is that? Then it followed most naturally, It is God that has made all. Well, but then, it came on, if God has made all these things, he guides and governs them all, and all things that concern them; for the power that could make all things, must certainly have power to guide and direct them; if so, nothing can happen in the great circuit of his works, either without his knowledge or appointment.

And if nothing happens without his knowledge, he knows that I am here, and am in this dreadful condition; and if nothing happens without his appointment, he has appointed all this to befall me. Nothing occurred to my thought, to contradict any of these conclusions; and therefore it rested upon me with the greatest force, that it must needs be that God had appointed all this to befall me; that I was brought to this miserable circumstance by his direction, he having the sole power, not of me only, but of everything that happens in the world.[8]

Crusoe then opens one of the chests that he took from the ship. He is after some tobacco to use in a medicinal concoction that he learned about in Brazil. But in the chest is a Bible. And the pages open to Psalm 50:15: "Call on Me in the day of trouble, and I will answer you and you will glorify Me."

That is the moment when Crusoe's transformation began to take effect. The next day he spent reading the New Testament. On that day, he turned his life completely over to Jesus Christ. And now that he knew that Christ was his personal Savior and Lord, he was immediately filled with hope! Here is how Robinson Crusoe describes the impact of the Bible on his life on that particular day:

This was the first time in all my life I could say, in the true sense of the words, that I prayed; for now I prayed with a sense of my condition, and with a true Scripture view of hope, founded on the encouragement of the word of God; and from this time, I may say, *I began to have hope that God would hear me.* (emphasis added)[9]

Now the next paragraph is priceless. In this next section, he describes a transformation that took place in his thinking that turned his desert into an oasis. As a reader, you begin to realize that this is exactly why God allowed Crusoe to end up in a pit. Up until the shipwreck, he was running *from* God. Now He is running *to* God.

> Now I began to construe the words mentioned above, "Call on Me and I will deliver thee," in a different sense from what I have ever done before; for then I had no notion of anything being called deliverance, but my being delivered from the captivity that I was in; for though I was indeed at large in the place, yet the island was certainly a prison to me, and that in the worst sense of the word. But now I learned to take it in another sense; I now looked back upon my past life with such horror, and my sins appeared so dreadful, that my soul sought nothing of God but deliverance from the load of guilt that bored down on all my comfort. As for my solitary life, it was nothing; I did not so much as pray to be delivered from it, or think of it; it was all of no consideration in comparison with this. *And I add this part here, to hint to whoever shall read it, that whenever they come to a true sense of things, they will find deliverance from affliction.*
>
> *My condition began now to be, though not less miserable as to my way of living, yet much easier to my mind; and my thoughts being directed, by constantly reading the Scriptures and praying to God, to things of a higher nature, I had a great deal of comfort within.*[10]

Do you see what has taken place in this young man's life? He is in the pit, he is stranded on an island with little, if any, possibility that he will ever be rescued. But in the middle of this biggest of all trapdoor experiences, he suddenly comes to a place of acceptance. And not just a place of acceptance.

He is at a place of perfect rest. He is okay with his life. He is okay with the fact that he's in the pit. He has gotten closure and resolution to his circumstances, even though his circumstances didn't change one iota.

So what happened?

He saw that the hand of a sovereign God was providentially behind his circumstances. The God who loved him, died for him, and had his best interests in mind had put him on that island. And once he got a grip on that, it changed *everything*.

No, he didn't get an e-mail that, through a GPS satellite, the Coast Guard had discovered his position and a chopper was on the way. He didn't meet a beautiful woman who would, from that day on, be his loving and caring companion on the island. None of that happened. Not one negative circumstance changed, yet *he* changed. It all had to do with his perspective of God. He suddenly realized that God was in absolute control of his life.

It was God who had put him on that island for his good. And when it was in his best interests to get off the island, God would do that as well. Several years ago, there was a best-selling book by the title *Thriving on Chaos*. Our lives do at times get so hectic and chaotic that it's all we can do to keep our heads above water. But there is another perspective to the events that we find ourselves swimming in. That other perspective could easily be called *Thriving on Providence*. What appears to be chaotic is all under the hand, control, and power of almighty God.

Listen, if Jesus Christ is your Lord and Savior, there is no chaos in your life. There may be stress, difficulties, hardships, disappointments, and problems. But things are not spinning out of control. He is in absolute control of your circumstances and the events of your life.

"There are three things in God's providence: God's foreknowing, God's determining, and God's directing all things to their periods and events."[11] This is precisely what Robinson Crusoe realized as he sat and pondered the fact that he was marooned on an island.

Are you in the pit?

Do you feel marooned in some nagging, heartbreaking crisis in your life? Then you must reason the same way that Crusoe did. You must come to the point where you can say this: "God allowed me to get into these circumstances for a reason that will somehow shake out for my good. Nothing is bigger than God, and nothing can stop God doing good for me and to me. If God has me in a pit, it's because He's going to somehow work this pit for my good."

Chuck Smith, the founding pastor of Calvary Chapel, is worth hearing when he writes on the issue of faith and character being hammered out in the heat of trials.

One of the secrets of my preparation for this work, I am convinced, was my desert years, those years of struggle. It was in this crucible, I believe, that God prepared my character for the coming work....

I have learned from all these things that God is working out a fore-ordained, prearranged plan. He is directing every turn and facet of my life, if I will only look to Him for guidance. Sometimes, because I do not understand the difficulty I am facing, I must look through the eyes of faith. And through faith I must realize that all things are working together for good. But then as I look back I can see that the hand of God was leading me and directing me into various things. It is so beautiful to trace His hand in my life—even though sometimes He was directing me into a move that was not an easy or comfortable situation, but He needed to teach me some lessons.

Sometimes when I moved, God was teaching me not to move without being directed. And so He let me make that move to show me the danger of going ahead without His direction. But even then I can see the hand of God as He was working out His perfect plan in my life. He knew what it would take to bring me to Himself, He knew the circumstances it would take to bring me to a complete commitment of myself to Him. And then He knew what it would take to bring me to the end of myself, where I would give up totally and completely, reckoning my old self to be dead. And God knew exactly what it would take, circumstantially, to bring this transition in my life.

God also knew the work He planned to do through me to touch the lives of others. He knew and foreordained the work I was to accomplish for His glory that would have a rippling effect until it reached around the world. Before He could work through me, He had to work in me, conforming me by His Spirit into His image, bringing me into the measure of the stature of the fullness of Christ. Once He had accomplished His work in me, He could then do all of those things He was desiring to do through me.

I do not believe that I have fully apprehended that for which He appointed me, nor do I feel His work in my own character is complete. I still have a long way to go before I fully reflect the image of Christ! But thank God His work continues as He is changing me from glory to glory.[12]

God had some great things in mind for Chuck Smith to do. But first there had to be a long season of preparation in his life.

He had to spend some time on the deserted island.

He had to log some days at Engedi.

He had to seek the Lord from the bottom of a pit.

Preparation always includes time in the pit. God had in mind some great things for David to do. But first he had to be prepared in the pit.

That's why David was running for his life. That's why he was afraid to sleep twice in the same place. He had to keep moving. He had to hide away. And that's why he headed for Engedi.

The question is why? If God has chosen David to be the next king of Israel, why didn't He just go ahead and bump Saul and put David on the throne? Why did David have to go through all those agonizing years on the run, in terror for his very life? Wasn't there an easier way to transition from one king to another? This was tougher than waiting for the hanging chads to be counted in Florida.

Why would God require David to experience those years of trouble at all? If He was truly David's Friend, why didn't He step in and put an end to it somehow?...

In the first place, it may have been that David's friendship with God had reached a plateau—a leveling off point. It is almost a truism that nothing in the spiritual life remains level. There is either an advance or a decline. If David was going to go on in his relationship with God, he had to experience God's grace in a deeper way. For that reason, in His love, the Lord allowed David to enter a time of trial. No one really advances in his walk with God in a time of complete tranquility. No one develops muscles of faith and trust when everything is prosperity and peace. David's years as a fugitive brought him to the end of himself. And once he reached the limits of wisdom and endurance, David found resources beyond anything he had ever experienced. He began to tap the infinite resources of God, resources he would sorely need as the king of Israel![13]

Robinson Crusoe was not advancing with God. He was rapidly declining. Like David, he needed to experience the grace of God in a way that would change his heart and enable him to grow in a relationship with the Lord. In order to rescue Crusoe from a rebellious and hardened heart, God used the shipwreck to pull the trapdoor on Robinson and put him on the island. That shipwreck was an unscheduled pit stop.

The great evangelist of the 18th century George Whitefield was once robbed in such a way that it spoke of the goodness of God.

Once when he was riding to a meeting with another man, a robber met them on the road and demanded all their money. The cocked pistol in his hand was argument enough, and the two did as the robber insisted. The robber left and the two continued on. In a few moments, the robber returned and demanded Whitefield's coat, saying, "It is better than mine." Once again, the preacher did as he was told. With a smirk, the thief threw his old coat to Whitefield and rode away again.

As Whitefield and his friend continued on their journey, they looked behind them only to see the robber riding at full gallop toward them again. Deciding enough was enough, the two spurred their horses and reached the next town safely before the robber reached them. Later they wondered why the thief tried to get them a third time, but when Whitefield felt the lining of the thief's coat, he found the answer: Inside was a purse with many times more money in it than the thief had taken.[14] Whitefield used the money for the orphans that he supported in Georgia.

It was John Flavel who said, "Some providences, like Hebrew letters, must be read backwards." In some instances you can't see the goodness of God until you get on down the trail and look back.

Was it the goodness of God for Whitefield to be staring down the barrel of a pistol held by a very dangerous man? At that immediate moment, it would have been very, very easy to question the goodness of God. But later that day, when Whitefield discovered the money in the thief's coat, there was no question of the goodness of God. Sometimes the providence of God must be read backwards. What doesn't look at first like His goodness, will one day prove to be the goodness of God.

What have you been robbed of? Your health? Your career? Perhaps your children have been taken from you to live in another home. Perhaps someone has robbed you of your reputation by telling lies about you in an effort to destroy you. We can be robbed of a hundred different things, some not so painful, others so painful to a degree that all we can do is scream silently inside.

If you are in the pit, you have suffered some kind of great loss. Somebody took your coat, somebody took your comfort. And with a sarcastic laugh, they threw you a rag that used to be a coat.

The providence of God means that somewhere in that coat of circumstances, hidden in the lining, is the wealth of the goodness of God. Sure, you can't see it now. You may not even be able to feel it. But it's there. The goodness of God is always there. And his provision is always exactly on time.

Somewhere in your pit is an oasis.

Somewhere in your pit is an Engedi.

And somewhere in that tattered, fraying coat of circumstance is a check made out to you that is drawn on the Bank of the Goodness of God. How much is it for? I don't know the amount, but it's bigger than what you lost. Much bigger.

He "is able to do far more abundantly beyond all that we ask or think" (Ephesians 3:20).

Now there's a promise you can take straight to the bank.

FOUR

THE BATTLE
OF ALL BATTLES

*The Kingdom of God advances through a series of glorious victories
cleverly disguised as disasters.*

ANONYMOUS

FREDERIC REMINGTON IS FAMOUS FOR HIS PAINTINGS and sculptures of the Old West. But as a young man, he worked as an illustrator for William Randolph Hearst, the most powerful media man in the world.

Hearst owned newspapers across the country, and his power and influence were legendary. In August of 1897, Hearst sent Remington on a special assignment to Cuba to cover the impending war between the rebels and the government. When Remington arrived with famous journalist Richard Harding Davis, they traveled all over Cuba looking for unrest. But they couldn't find any.

Remington decided to head back to America. So he cabled William Randolph Hearst: *"Everything is quiet. There is no trouble. There will be no war. I wish to return."*

Hearst wired him back: *"Please remain. You furnish the pictures and I'll furnish the war."*[1]

The statement is attributed to Hearst, but the one who actually furnished a war may have been Franklin Delano Roosevelt, some forty years later.

It appeared that FDR had a major problem on his hands when the Japanese attacked Pearl Harbor on December 7, 1941. But the president's biggest problem wasn't declaring war on Japan; it was forcing and manipulating Japan to attack Pearl Harbor in the first place.

You may want to go back and read that sentence again to make sure you got it right. But you did. I've been reading a fascinating book by Robert B. Stinnett called *Day of Deceit: The Truth about FDR and Pearl Harbor*. In case you think right out of the blocks that this is some kind of nutso-conspiracy-theory book (as I did), you should know that the book has been lauded by publications such as the *Wall Street Journal, The New York Times,* and the *Chicago Sun-Times.*

Tom Roesser, writing for the *Chicago Sun-Times,* stated: "Stinnett has made a sickening discovery through the Freedom of Information Act....FDR must have known... *Day of Deceit* is perhaps the most revelatory document of our time."

John Attarian of *The Detroit News* wrote, "Backed by seventeen years of research and using more that two hundred thousand interviews and newly classified documents, Stinnett makes devastating revelations.... He is a model researcher."[2]

I realize you probably haven't read Stinnett's book. But as crazy as it may sound, let's assume for a minute he's correct. The obvious question then would be *why?* Why would Franklin Delano Roosevelt want Japan to attack Pearl Harbor?

In 1940–41, Americans did not want to enter the war with Hitler. Polling data back then wasn't an everyday occurrence, but polls consistently showed that 88 percent of all Americans did not want to get into another war. That was an amazingly high number that didn't vary.

> Roosevelt believed that provoking Japan into an attack on Hawaii was the only option he had in 1941 to overcome the powerful America First non-interventionist movement led by aviation hero Charles Lindbergh. These anti-war views were shared by 80 percent of the American public from 1940 to 1941. Though Germany had conquered most of Europe, and her U-Boats were sinking American ships in the Atlantic Ocean—including warships—Americans wanted nothing to do with "Europe's War."[3]

Stinnett points out that, sixty years later, it's hard for us to understand just how strong the isolationist movement was in that era. It was led by Charles Lindbergh, one of America's greatest heroes. He had incredible influence not only in America, but across the world. And he was leading the charge for America to stay out of the war. The conflict, Lindbergh reasoned, was between Hitler and Churchill. If Germany wanted to rule Europe, well, that was up to them. But America should stay out of it. But here is where it got very interesting:

Germany made a strategic error. She, along with her Axis partner, Italy, signed the mutual assistance treaty with Japan, the Tripartite Pact, on September 27, 1940. Ten days later, Lieutenant Commander Arthur McCollum, a U.S. Naval officer in the Office of Naval Intelligence (ONI), saw an opportunity to counter the U.S. isolationist movement by provoking Japan into a state of war with the U.S., triggering the mutual assistance provisions of the Tripartite Pact, and bringing America into World War II.

Memorialized in McCollum's secret memo dated October 7, 1940, and recently obtained through the Freedom of Information Act, the ONI proposal called for eight provocations aimed at Japan. Its centerpiece was keeping the might of the U.S. Fleet based in the Territory of Hawaii as a lure for a Japanese attack.[4]

Stinnett then fills in the rest:

Eight steps were suggested to provoke a Japanese attack. Shortly after reviewing them, Roosevelt put them into effect. After the eighth provocation had been taken, Japan responded. On November 27 and 28, 1941, U.S. military commanders were given this order: "The United States desires that Japan commit the first overt act." According to Secretary of War Henry L. Stinson, the order came directly from President Roosevelt.

There has been a controversy over American foreknowledge of the events of December 7, 1941. We have long known that Japanese diplomatic cables—which pointed toward hostilities—were intercepted and decoded. What I have discovered, however, is that we knew much more. Not only did we undertake provocative steps, we intercepted and decoded military cables. We knew the attack was coming."[5]

As we all know, on December 8th, millions of young Americans flooded recruiting stations—Marine and Army and Navy—and joined the military. Civilians went to work and produced the huge war machine that eventually defeated Japan *and* Hitler—who was really the main target.[6]

Roosevelt was afraid that if America waited to get into the war until after Hitler had defeated England, it would be too late.

Through thousands of intelligence documents that had been spirited away for safekeeping in military vaults, Stinnett uncovered what history had kept hidden. The biggest battle facing Franklin Delano Roosevelt was not fighting Japan and Germany. Roosevelt's toughest battle was raising the American people out of their apathy before it was too late. *That* was the battle. Quite frankly, Roosevelt had to go to battle with people he loved and promised to serve.[7]

So what is the moral of this story?

The moral is that what appears to be your biggest battle, may not be your hardest battle after all.

That's the very clear message of Psalm 77. Here's an intelligence document that is not hidden away in some dusty vault. It can easily be found in your Bible. And this document will clue you in on the biggest battle you will ever fight in your life.

LIFE IN THE BULL'S-EYE

Some of you are in a battle right now. And you're thinking that it's the battle of all battles. You might be fighting to keep your marriage alive. You might be fighting against alcohol or pornography. Maybe one of your kids has gotten hooked on drugs and you're fighting with every ounce of strength and emotional energy within you to save this child who got off track. Those are all huge battles. They are life-and-death struggles that rip your guts out.

We battle the world, the flesh, and the devil, and none of these battles are for the faint of heart. When a man gives his life to Christ and follows Him passionately and wholeheartedly, that is the man who has a bull's-eye painted on his back. When Satan and his demons observe a man who is sold out to Christ, they line that man up in their crosshairs and begin to fire at everything and anything in his life. The enemy is cruel, relentless, and vicious.

But as big and difficult as such battles may be, there is a war front far bigger and far more serious. There is more at stake in this battle than in any other battle you will ever face in your life.

The battle of which I speak, like Roosevelt's battle, is a secret—covered up by circumstances and hidden away in the vaults of denial. And it is a battle against someone you love.

The battle of all battles is when you find yourself battling God. Tune in for a few minutes to the emotional, first person account of a man who found himself in that very struggle. His name was Asaph, and his deeply personal story is recorded for us in Psalm 77.

My voice rises to God, and I will cry aloud;
My voice rises to God, and He will hear me.
In the day of my trouble I sought the Lord;
In the night my hand was stretched out without weariness;
My soul refused to be comforted.
When I remember God, then I am disturbed;
When I sigh, then my spirit grows faint. Selah.
You have held my eyelids open;
I am so troubled that I cannot speak.
I have considered the days of old,
The years of long ago.
I will remember my song in the night;
I will meditate with my heart,
And my spirit ponders:
Will the Lord reject forever?
And will He never be favorable again?

Has His lovingkindness ceased forever?
Has His promise come to an end forever?
Has God forgotten to be gracious,
Or has He in anger withdrawn His compassion? Selah.
Then I said, "It is my grief,
That the right hand of the Most High has changed."
I shall remember the deeds of the LORD;
Surely I will remember Your wonders of old.
I will meditate on all Your work
And muse on Your deeds.
Your way, O God, is holy;
What god is great like our God?
You are the God who works wonders;
You have made known Your strength among the peoples.
You have by Your power redeemed Your people,
The sons of Jacob and Joseph. Selah.
The waters saw You, O God;
The waters saw You, they were in anguish;
The deeps also trembled.
The clouds poured out water;
The skies gave forth a sound;
Your arrows flashed here and there.
The sound of Your thunder was in the whirlwind;
The lightnings lit up the world;
The earth trembled and shook.
Your way was in the sea
And Your paths in the mighty waters,
And Your footprints may not be known.
You led Your people like a flock
By the hand of Moses and Aaron.

A DESPERATE CRY

We can never really know the exact circumstances behind this psalm. But we
do know this much. The writer is in trouble. Serious trouble. He finds him-

self in the heat and flames of a great trial and he is calling out to God in desperation.

I remember a day years ago when I cried out in desperation. It occurred at the home of my brother, Mike. My family was spending a few days with Mike's family, and we had just finished dinner. The four adults were going to go to a movie and were scrambling to clean up and get dressed after an afternoon of swimming. I'd just done a quick diaper change on Josh, who was about two at the time. I had walked back into the kitchen to get my wallet, picking my way through a maze of kids and toys. Between the two families, there were six kids running around and chaos galore.

Suddenly, I just stopped.

Where's Josh?

I don't know why that thought came to me right then. I'd just been with the little guy not a minute before. Kids were running and yelling all over the place, we were trying to get out the door, and in the midst of all that noise and activity, I was struck with the question, "Where is Josh?"

I looked around and didn't see him. I then noticed that the back door to the pool was slightly ajar. And then my eyes flashed to the pool—where I could see Josh at the bottom of the deep end. As I went flying out the door, I yelled at the top of my lungs, *"MIKE!"*

I didn't know where Mike was in the house, but I knew he would hear my voice. I dove straight into the pool, clothes and all, reached down to the bottom, grabbed Josh, shot up as fast as I could to the surface, and held him with one arm above the water. Mike was right there to grab him as I broke the surface.

Josh spit out water and started crying.

Then I spit out water and started crying.

It was the Holy Spirit who prompted me as I walking down that noisy and crowded hallway. And when I realized the utter severity of the situation, I cried out. And fortunately, Mike heard my voice.

That's exactly what is happening in verse 1.

Only, there is a difference. I knew that Mike was somewhere in the house—and that he would be right behind me. I knew in that moment that we would connect. I just knew it.

But the guy in Psalm 77 doesn't have that same assurance. He's battling to connect with God, because God has allowed him to get into some very harsh circumstances.

Verse 2 describes a man in turmoil and pain.

> In the day of my trouble I sought the Lord;
> In the night my hand was stretched out without weariness;
> My soul refused to be comforted.

Did you notice that he mentions the day and then in the next line speaks of the night? He's calling out night and day. He's going after God for help and for relief. But he is in dire straits. His soul refuses to be comforted.

John Knox was one of a handful of men God used to bring about the Reformation. Because of the work and preaching of men like Martin Luther, John Calvin, Ulrich Zwingli, and many others, the gospel was rescued from the false teachings of the medieval Roman Catholic church. These men trumpeted the truth that salvation is not by works or by doing penance, but is the free gift of Jesus Christ to everyone who believes on His name.

Six powerful words rang forth from the Reformation in the 1500s: *The just shall live by faith.* Many men died for their faith, including Zwingli. Luther, Calvin, and Knox were often in danger of torture or of being drawn and quartered.

John Knox, whom God used to bring about the Scottish reformation, was a Roman Catholic priest. Then he heard the message of the gospel and became associated with George Wishart, a strong Scottish preacher. Wishart had many enemies, and young Knox served as his bodyguard. When Wishart was arrested and burned at the stake, Knox became a fugitive. He took refuge in St. Andrews Castle, but it was soon conquered. And that's when John Knox became a slave. Not just any kind of slave, but a *galley* slave.

> Until the coming of the concentration camp, the galley held an undisputed preeminence as the darkest blot on Western Civilization; a galley, said a poetic observer shudderingly, would cast a shadow in the blackest midnight.[8]

The life of a galley slave was nothing short of pure hell on earth. For the convicts, of course, there was no question of sleep. Cooking facilities were primitive, and as no one ever washed, the ship crawled with vermin from stem to stern. From below came the constant clank of chains, the crack of whips on bare flesh, screams of pain, and savage growls. At each oar all five men had to rise as one at each stroke, push the eighteen-foot oar forward, dip it in the water, and pull with all their force, dropping into a sitting position at the end of each stroke. "One would not think," said a Huguenot convict, "that it was possible to keep it up for half an hour, and yet I have rowed full out for twenty hours without pausing for a single moment."9

That was John Knox's existence for nineteen months. Knox reflected on it as "a time of torment" and memories of it as the "sobs of his heart."10 Knox's time in the galley was a bitter gall that afflicted him physically for the rest of his life. He never fully recovered from his time on that French slave ship. You talk about night and day calling out to God! That was Knox in the galley. There had to be times when he battled to connect with God because of the overwhelming severity of his circumstances. There had to be times when he grappled with hopelessness and despair. I can lose perspective very quickly when I go two or three nights deprived of adequate sleep. Imagine how Knox had to battle! There had to be moments when his soul refused to be comforted. At those times, John Knox would have strongly identified with the writer of Psalm 77.

There are times in life

- when God is distant
- when God is silent
- when God is unresponsive

And that's precisely what Asaph is battling with in Psalm 77. Notice how he describes the intensity of his battle in verses 3–4:

When I remember God, then I am disturbed;
When I sigh, then my spirit grows faint.

You have held my eyelids open;
I am so troubled that I cannot speak.

This is the exact place where Job found himself after he had been stripped of everything:

"Behold, I go forward but He is not there,
And backward, but I cannot perceive Him;
When He acts on the left, I cannot behold Him;
He turns on the right, I cannot see Him." (Job 23:8–9)

There is no battle you will ever fight more difficult than this one. The battle to connect with God when everything is falling apart in your life is the most exhausting and trying conflict you will ever experience. And what makes it so hard is that God is supposed to *be there* for you when the walls close in on your life! He's supposed to *be there* when the trapdoor opens beneath your feet and you find yourself in that dark, loathsome pit. But He is nowhere to be found.

That's why Asaph says, "When I remember God, then I am disturbed...I am so troubled that I cannot speak." This guy is so frustrated and despairing that he can't even articulate everything that's going on down deep inside of him.

J. C. Penney was a man who wanted to do business God's way. The golden rule was young Mr. Penney's philosophy for doing business. Early in his career, his integrity was tested when he refused to get involved in a kickback scheme. Because of his refusal, his business was boycotted and he had to shut down and leave town. That's when an opportunity opened up in Wyoming. He started that store in 1907, with the help of a local businessman who believed in him. In just five years, he grew his business to thirty-four stores with sales of over $2 million. That was a lot of money in 1907.

He then moved the headquarters to New York and oversaw his company's incredible expansion. From 1917 to 1929, J. C. Penney's grew exponentially to 1400 stores across America. J. C. Penney was Sam Walton before Sam Walton ever came on the scene.

But Penney's public prosperity did not shield him from private hardship and suffering. Along this remarkable path of success, his first wife died in 1910, leaving him with two young sons. In his own words, "in that hour, my world crashed around me." Six years later, he married Mary Kimball, an editor for *The Christian Herald* magazine. Once again, Penney enjoyed the companionship and love of a faithful woman. But shortly after giving birth to their son, Kimball, Mary died in 1923. Once again, he was crushed beyond description.

And then in the crash of 1929, he personally lost $40 million. Penney found himself virtually penniless by 1932. It was too much for him to bear. With a broken heart and the loss of a fortune, he wound up as a patient in a sanatorium.[11]

In the life of J. C. Penney, God had become distant, silent, and unresponsive. When he remembered God, then he was disturbed. His soul refused to be comforted. He was in the pit, for the third time. He first wife was seized by death and so was his second. And then came the great crash that stripped James Cash Penney of all he had labored to build through the years. It was this third unscheduled pit stop that just about did him in. He thought he was finished. His health was nearly gone, his heart was broken, and his spirit was crushed. He was in an institution. His best days were behind him. He was fifty-six, almost fifty-seven. The same age as Winston Churchill when he was in that hospital bed in New York City. Both men had made unscheduled pit stops in their late 50s. They were starting from scratch, and neither one of them thought they would make it.

J. C. Penney was fighting the biggest battle of his life. And it wasn't to rebuild his empire. It was to regain his trust in the goodness of God.

But one morning, as he was dressing and fighting off depression, he heard some employees singing a hymn in the kitchen as they prepared breakfast:

Be not dismayed, what'er betide,
God will take care of you.

That one line from a popular hymn invaded the heart of J. C. Penney, and hope was reborn. God used that bit of verse to reconnect his heart to the Lord he thought had abandoned him. He recommitted his life to the Lord at that very moment. And at the age of fifty-six, he was ready to start from scratch, all over again.

God didn't leave J. C. Penney in the sanatorium.

He didn't leave Churchill in the hospital bed.

He didn't leave John Knox in the slave galley.

And He won't leave you, no matter where you are. But in the midst of the battle, sometimes it can sure seem that way.

BATTLING WRONG THOUGHTS

A British spy once sent a report back to England about the status of the thirteen colonies and their displeasure with the tax burden that King George had put upon them. In his report, he was briefing the king on the various colonial leaders. When it came to John Adams, the lawyer from Boston and future second president of the United States, he made this statement: "John Adams sees large things largely."[12]

When we do not understand God's dealings with us, we must attempt to see large things largely. God is a large subject and so are His ways. And if we think that we can understand His ways, we're going to be sorely disappointed. In fact, He clearly tells us there will be times when we certainly *won't* understand His dealings with us:

"For My thoughts are not your thoughts,
Neither are your ways My ways," declares the LORD.
"For as the heavens are higher than the earth,
So are My ways higher than your ways
And My thoughts than your thoughts." (Isaiah 55:8–9)

One of the great battles of the Christian life is to fight off wrong thinking about God when His ways don't make sense to us. When things go wrong, horribly wrong, and our hopes and dreams are smashed and pulverized, our first tendency is to begin thinking incorrectly about God.

There are two options before us when life falls apart: right thinking or wrong thinking.

One of the great treasures that John Adams left was his diary. He left an account of his life, written in his own hand, that gives us a running commentary on the events of his life.

In 1765 the brutal hammer of British taxation threatened to crush citizens of the colonies. John Adams, at the age of thirty, wrote an essay that spread like wildfire through young America. People were taken with the wisdom of his argument and the clarity of his comments about the divine rights that had been given to the citizens of each colony. It was an essay that had been very carefully thought out.

John Adams spent a lot of his time thinking. How do I know it? It's in his diary.

"The year 1765 has been the most remarkable year of my life," Adams penned. "At home with my family. Thinking," reads the entry of a few nights later.

"At home. Thinking." he wrote Christmas Day.[13]

But Adams wasn't just thinking. He was thinking largely.

In Psalm 77, in verses 7–10, Asaph is just about overcome by his circumstances. Something catastrophic has happened to him that makes him ask a series of tortured, haunting questions:

Will the Lord reject forever?
And will He never be favorable again?
Has His lovingkindness ceased forever?
Has His promise come to an end forever?
Has God forgotten to be gracious,
Or has He in anger withdrawn His compassion?
Then I said, "It is my grief,
That the right hand of the Most High has changed."

Maybe you find yourself in a situation where you've been asking similar questions. From all appearances, God has taken off on a long trip and left His cell phone turned off.

God is distant.

God is silent.

God is unresponsive.

I remember years ago sitting on my front porch trying to absorb the biggest ministry setback of my life. I had put everything into this venture. I had given it all my effort, all my energy, and now it was utterly destroyed. I'm talking total annihilation. In one afternoon, the whole thing went down. As I sat on the porch that night, I was absolutely devastated. I was battling God and I was battling wrong thoughts about God. I was feeling utterly abandoned by God. And quite frankly, I was angry at Him, because ultimately, I knew He was the One who had allowed this great ministry plan of mine to come unraveled.

But if I could have had a glimpse at that moment of what God had in store for me over the next ten years, I would have been on my knees thanking and praising Him for His goodness and lovingkindness in allowing my plan to die. God killed my dream because He had a better plan. He had something else for me to do. I must confess that I was not thinking largely about God that night. I was thinking cockeyed because I didn't understand His ways.

God is good even when our dreams and plans are nuked beyond recognition. But you must think largely and correctly to get a grip on your circumstances when your dreams and plans are going up in smoke.

In verse 10, Asaph begins to think largely. And that's what pulls him out of the funk.

BATTLING TO REMEMBER!

"Remember Pearl Harbor!" That was the battle cry that kept America's troops and citizens motivated throughout World War II. If Roosevelt did manipulate circumstances to force the Japanese into the attack, he got more mileage out of it than he could have dared hope. Not only did the attack infuriate America out of its passivity, but the remembrance of Pearl Harbor kept morale high even through the darkest days of the war.

When God is distant, when He is silent, and when He is unresponsive, the great battle you must fight and win is to remember what He has done for you in the past. That's the battle Asaph is waging in verses 11–15. I have taken the liberty of putting some key words in italics:

I shall *remember* the deeds of the LORD;
Surely I will *remember* Your wonders of old.
I will *meditate* on all Your work
And *muse* on Your deeds.
Your way, O God, is holy;
What god is great like our God?
You are the God who works wonders;
You have made known Your strength among the peoples.
You have by Your power redeemed Your people,
The sons of Jacob and Joseph. Selah.

There will be times along the trail when it seems that God is hiding from you. When He does that (and at some point He will), it is an action that He takes for our good. There is something He wants to achieve in our lives, and it requires Him to seemingly withdraw (although He has not withdrawn at all). He knows precisely what He is doing, He has His eye upon us, and His good steady hand is as present as it has always been. We just don't sense it. And we don't see it.

When God is apparently inactive in the present, we must remember what He has done in the past. You see it right there in Psalm 77. And it is there for a reason. God had Asaph write these words so that we would have a template to follow when we get in the same kind of fix Asaph was in. There is a model that is intended here—a formula. And the formula is about as simple as it could possibly be.

Remember.

But our memories can be very fickle. We tend to remember the bad things and forget the great things. Psalm 103:2 says, "Bless the LORD, O my soul, and *forget* none of His benefits." But that is precisely what we tend to do. We tend not to remember His benefits; for whatever reason, we never call them to mind.

It was Charles Haddon Spurgeon who observed that "memory is very treacherous about the best things; by a strange perversity...it treasures up the refuse of the past and permits priceless treasures to lie neglected."[14]

What priceless treasures of God's goodness have you neglected and failed to remember? If you know Christ, you have them. You can look back over your life and see the good hand of God at work. There were times when He came through for you at the last possible second and rescued you. There were times when you thought all was lost, and it wasn't. God has been very, very gracious to you and me—but how quickly we forget.

We can't forget! We can't afford to have selective memories! The enemy wants us to get so down and discouraged that we develop selective memories and forget all of His benefits. But at critical junctures in life, you can't forget. You have to stir yourself up and think largely! Get out the wide-angle lens and go back over the big picture and see and remember what He has done. That will help you turn the corner. That will be the pivot that will enable you to get your feet back under you. Remember!

And when you mentally go back over your life and begin to think largely, something big, something major that God has done will suddenly emerge from the dark tunnel of your present circumstances and hardships. Like a Los Angeles-class submarine surfacing out of the deep, some great thing that God has done will come shooting to the surface and remind you of His great and breathtaking power.

That's precisely what happened to Asaph. As he is remembering the past, he suddenly hits on a key event that knocks him over with the power and goodness of God. What he remembers in verses 16–20 is the Red Sea:

> The waters saw You, O God;
> The waters saw You, they were in anguish;
> The deeps also trembled.
> The clouds poured out water;
> The skies gave forth a sound;
> Your arrows flashed here and there.
> The sound of Your thunder was in the whirlwind;
> The lightnings lit up the world;
> The earth trembled and shook.
> Your way was in the sea
> And Your paths in the mighty waters,
> And Your footprints may not be known.

You led Your people like a flock
By the hand of Moses and Aaron.

There is a lesson that comes through loud and clear by remembering the day that God parted the sea to save the people of Israel: *God will go to any extreme to direct, guide, and protect His people.*

But one thing must be added to that principle: *He will do it on His timetable, not yours.*

That's the lesson that you will have to fight to remember. When you are battling the worst of circumstances in the present, at the same time you must battle to remember the goodness of God in the past.

A statue of Winston Churchill stands in front of the British Embassy in Washington, D.C.—a fitting tribute to the great statesman who led Britain to victory in her finest hour. In the early years of the war, however, Churchill was fighting alone—many Americans wanted no part of that war. Some people don't realize that Churchill could claim both countries as his own; his father was English, but his mother was an American. Because of his unique status the statue in front of the British Consulate is uniquely positioned. It was laid in place so that one of Churchill's feet would be on the property of the British Consulate, but the other foot reaches across the property line and stands on American soil.

That's precisely how we must battle when God seems distant. We fight with one foot in the present, battling the wrong thoughts that Satan would throw against us. But we win that battle by having one foot in the past, remembering what God has done for us in days gone by. If He led us in the past, He will lead us in the present. If He rescued us in the past, He will rescue us now.

"Remember Pearl Harbor" worked in World War II as they fought the battle for their very survival. "Remember the Red Sea" worked for Asaph as he battled.

Those were large events. And God has done something—many things—large for you in the past as well.

Remember it! And remember it largely.

FIVE

CAREER INTERRUPTIONS

It is time I stepped aside for a less experienced and less able man.

PROFESSOR SCOTT ELLEDGE, ON HIS RETIREMENT FROM CORNELL

I WRITE THESE OPENING PARAGRAPHS ON SEPT 22, 2001. This chapter was done and in the can on September 10. But on the morning of September 11, just eleven days ago today, things changed.

In fact, *everything* changed.

Prior to the eleventh, our national economy was in something of a mild recession. The previous nine months had seen a large number of layoffs. Guys who, a year before, had been making good salaries found themselves hoping to scrape enough together to make their mortgage payment. But there was hope that things were beginning to turn around. Because I knew so many guys here in Dallas and around the country who had lost their jobs or were just "stuck" in their careers, I pulled together this chapter to encourage them that God was working in them—building steel into their souls even in the pressure and heat of their circumstances.

And then the terrorists hit the World Trade Center in their commandeered Boeings. And life as we know it in this nation will never be the same again. That doesn't mean it will all be doom and gloom. It won't, if you know the Lord and you are following Him. But if you don't know Him—or if you do know Him and you're lax in your personal application of the truth—then let me just go ahead and put something on the table.

Your future doesn't look too promising.

And the sooner you come to that realization, the better off you will be.

Before September 11, I had six principles about our careers and work out of Psalm 75 that I wanted to cover in this chapter. I'll go ahead and lay out Psalm 75 and even give you the principles. But this chapter has expanded to two chapters, and we won't even begin to discuss the key points until the next chapter. Nevertheless, here are the principles:

Principle#1: Ultimately, all promotion is from the Lord.
Principle#2: When God is ready to promote you, no person, no group, no superior, no human network can stand in His way.
Principle#3: Ultimately, all layoffs are from the Lord.
Principle#4: When God is ready to lay you off, no person, no group, no superior, no human network can stand in His way.
Principle#5: God will test you before He promotes you.
Principle #6: God will lay you off to test you.

I've drawn all these points out of Psalm 75:6–7:

For neither from the east nor from the west nor from the desert does
    promotion come;
But God is the Judge. He puts down one and promotes another.
    (MLB)

But before we dig into those principles, we really need to talk.

THE AFTERMATH

In the last ten days since the Pentagon was attacked and the twin towers went down in flames in the heart of New York's financial district, there have been 200,000 layoffs in corporate America. In the airline industry alone, Boeing, American, Delta, Northwest, and Continental have laid off over 100,000. And that's just in the last week and a half.

The front page of the *Dallas Morning News* contained a graphic showing the stock market drop over the last week as being the single biggest in history. In blazing color the graphics demonstrated that the market drop this week surpassed the one of October 19–23, 1987—and even exceeded the plunge of October 28–November 1, 1929. That's the Great Depression. And we broke the record this week by seeing the stock market go down 14.3 percent. In 1929 it only went down 9.2 percent.

In a matter of days, this chapter has become increasingly more relevant to all of us. Maybe you've already been laid off. Perhaps you're thinking you may be laid off. Maybe you own your own business and you're wondering if you'll even *be* in business six months from now. If you're one of the fortunate in this country, you'll be able to hang on to your job in the weeks and months ahead.

One of my favorite writers is Peggy Noonan. Besides being practical and wise, this woman is simply brilliant. Back in 1998, she wrote an article that verged on the prophetic. I'm going to quote from her several times in this chapter. If you're a little tired and fuzzy-minded right now, I urge you to close this book and come back to it when you've had some rest. This is too important to let exhaustion block it from your head and heart.

Remember now, she wrote this piece back in 1998. Think for a minute what you were doing in 1998. The stock market was soaring, and the economy was roaring. The dot-coms were going through the roof. Some were predicting that the Dow would eventually hit 30,000. And in the midst of all those seemingly endless good times, she penned these words:

> The moment we are having is an awfully good one, though. History has handed us one of the easiest rides in all the story of man. It has handed us a wave of wealth so broad and deep that it would be almost disorienting if we thought about it a lot, which we don't.
>
> Lately this leaves me uneasy. Does it you? Do you wonder how and why exactly we have it so different, so nice compared to thousands of years of peasants eating rocks? Is it possible that we, the people of the world, are being given a last great gift before everything changes? To me it feels like a gift. Only three generations ago, my family had to sweat in the sun to pull food from the ground.[1]

Unless you happen to be a farmer, you're probably not pulling food up out of the ground. At least, not yet. (But planting a garden is never a bad idea.)

Tempered Steel is the title of this book. There is a reason for that. Life throws any number of varied challenges and hardships at us as we move along the trail of life. Everyone has his or her own unique set of difficulties. Some people deal with cancer, but not everyone. Some go through a divorce, remarry, and try to make sense of a blended family. But that's not everyone's experience. Some seem plagued by financial trouble that they can never quite shake. But once again, that's not the experience of everyone. Any one of those varied hardships will make you ask the question, "How will I ever survive the heat of these crushing circumstances?"

TROUBLE IN PARADISE?

But there is one pit I've noticed over the years that just about every man stumbles into at one time or another: losing a job. It might have been a firing, it might have been a corporate layoff, it might have been a merger that eliminated your position. However it comes about, if you're like most men you'll find yourself out of work at some point in your life.

And when that happens the question becomes, "How will I ever get through this?"

I live in the Dallas-Fort Worth metroplex. When I picked up the *Dallas Morning News* this morning, a headline on the front page caught my eye. It read, "Plano 75093: Trouble in Paradise?" So what's the trouble in this affluent suburb just north of Dallas?

Perched on the western edge of Plano, ZIP code 75093 would be an inviting place to live for almost anyone.

It harbors a lavish new mall, The Shops at Willow Bend, and lists more than a few high-profile property owners, including former Dallas Cowboys Troy Aikman and Deion Sanders.

It is home to prominent country clubs...and offers well-appointed houses, the majority of which range from $250,000 to a peak of $6.5 million....

The schools are exemplary, the restaurants superb, but there's a problem. Scores of residents, including corporate executives, managers, and consultants, are out of work, offering first-proof that the high-tech bubble has burst.... From January through July, Plano suffered a sharper rise in the number of unemployed than any city in the Dallas-Fort Worth area....

In January, 2,475 Plano residents were receiving unemployment benefits. By July, the number had more than doubled to 5,402.... Across the Dallas metropolitan area, more than 42,000 people have lost their jobs since January (2001).[2]

That article was written a couple of weeks before the terrorists hit the Pentagon and the World Trade Center. In other words, what the newspaper article described was "the good old days."

Men and women are living out that Plano story in cities and towns all over America. And it's not just the high-rent, upper-class neighborhoods feeling the pinch. Hardworking blue-collar folks are hurting as well. Plants and factories have been laying off people in droves all over this nation.

It doesn't matter what kind of work you do. It doesn't matter if you live in the penthouse or if you build penthouses, it still hurts, and it hurts bad, to be out of a job. Layoffs are the stuff that adds acid to our stomachs, pains to our chest, and worry and sleeplessness to our nights.

For most men there is more to a layoff than loss of income. There is an accompanying loss of self esteem, self worth, and self-respect. For most of us, those things are very closely tied to *what we do*. Men, in particular, feel a tremendous self-imposed pressure to be successful; to make it, to be ahead of the pack. No one wants to be ordinary. Terry Hershey writes, "We live in a world where more is never enough. Coping mechanisms and consequences are evident. We cannot be content, so we fantasize about those who 'arrive' by reading about lifestyles of rich and famous people; we sacrifice the values of our 'ordinary life' of relationships, family, and personal solitude to pursue the ecstasy that will let us 'be somebody.'"[3]

Hershey underlines an emphasis he keeps seeing in the media. The line goes like this: "If you're living life right, you're in ecstasy most of the time." And the only way to have a shot at ecstasy is to have the right career. Without the right career, it's nearly impossible to get your ticket to success, significance, and serious income.

An attorney who practices in Denver recently put it in these words:

Our professions have become very important to us and we're willing to perhaps sacrifice other things for them—marriages, families, free time, relaxation. Our marriages seems like mergers, our divorces like divestitures. (I have) gone through a number of important relationships which have failed because my commitment to my job was greater than my commitment to the relationship. If it was a toss-up between getting the deal done and coming home for supper, the deal got done.[4]

Let's face it. There are times when everyone has to work late. It's part of the curse that fell on Adam in the Garden. But that's not the issue this guy is talking about. He's endorsing a lifestyle that *consistently and purposefully* chooses career and business over personal relationships. If you're going to be successful, the reasoning goes, sacrificing spouses and children is just the cost of doing business. Why would anyone be willing to make such sacrifices to be successful? The answer is simple. Our culture believes that there is only one place to find true happiness and that is the place of success.

Anthony Campolo has written that:

Success is a shining city, a pot of gold at the end of the rainbow. We dream of it as children, we strive for it through our adult lives, and we suffer melancholy in old age if we have not reached it. *Success is the place of happiness.* And the anxieties we suffer at the thought of not arriving there give us ulcers, heart attacks, and nervous disorders. If our reach exceeds our grasp, and we fail to achieve what we want, life seems meaningless and we feel emotionally dead.[5]

That's why we're so stressed-out, so pressured. We can live with almost anything except the thought of not being successful. And it's killing us. That's why we have no time for anything else.

Suddenly, all over America, guys who had no time find themselves with nothing but time. That's what happens when you're out of work. Sure, you're updating your résumé and making calls, but after the first few weeks and the first hundred phone calls, you've got more free time than you could have ever imagined. Or wanted.

Why do you have so much free time? And why is it possible that this unemployment chapter may be an extended one? We are at war. Our nation has been attacked. More people were killed on the morning of September 11 than the total number of Americans killed in the entire Revolutionary War.

It's beginning to dawn on all of us that we may be in for a protracted war. We will be taking casualties at home and abroad. We're also in a time of recession. Deep recession. And it may go into the "D" word, depression. That hits a man right where he lives—because it's our job to provide for our families financially. There are some very serious ramifications of a wartime economy.

In the days ahead, very few men are going to be promoted.

In the days ahead, a significant number of men are going to experience layoffs.

In the days ahead, the vast majority of men will simply plateau in their careers—and consider themselves lucky! Why will they consider themselves fortunate? Because the unthinkable happened ten days ago. And in our guts, we all know that the Trade Center kamikazes were only the first shot fired across the bow. There will be more to come. Much more.

Remarkably, Noonan saw this and published her thoughts in *Forbes* back in 1998.

What will happen? How will the future play out?

Well, we're going to get more time. But it's not pretty how it will happen.... I mean: We live in a world of three billion men and hundreds of thousands of nuclear bombs, missiles, warheads. It's a world of extraordinary germs that can be harnessed and used to kill whole populations, a world of extraordinary chemicals that can be harnessed and used to do the same.

Three billion men, and it takes only half a dozen bright and evil ones to harness and deploy.

What are the odds it will happen? Put it another way: What are the odds it will not? Low. Nonexistent, I think.

She was right. And it has happened. Not only has the unimaginable taken place, but the enemy is living among us, and even as we read these pages they're using their evil imaginations to cripple, kill, maim, and infect as many Americans as they possibly can. This can't be real! But it is. And it will, in some shape or form, affect every single one of us reading these pages. But I must give you one more shot from Noonan's 1998 essay:

> When you consider who is gifted and crazed with rage…when you think of the terrorist places and the terrorist countries…who do they hate most? The Great Satan, the United States. What is its most important place? Some would say Washington. I would say the great city of the United States is the great city of the world, the dense 10-mile-long island called Manhattan, where the economic and media power of the nation resides, the city that is the psychological center of our modernity, our hedonism, our creativity, our hard-shouldered hipness, our unthinking arrogance.
>
> If someone does the big, terrible thing to New York or Washington, there will be a lot of chaos and a lot of lines going down, a lot of damage, and a lot of things won't be working so well anymore. And thus a lot more…time. Something tells me we won't be teleconferencing and faxing about the Ford account for a while.

Peggy Noonan wrote that column in September of 1998. What she thought might happen actually came to pass on September 11, 2001. And as you know, and as she guessed, it hit New York City and Washington, D.C. But everyone else in America is feeling the aftershocks. We're feeling them emotionally and we're feeling them economically. And this is probably just the first hit of many to come.

Thousands have lost loved ones.

Hundreds of thousands will lose jobs.

And if you're one of those hundreds of thousands, you might want to pause right now and thank God that you are not in the previous group. You may have lost a job, but you haven't lost a wife or a son or a daughter or a close friend. With God's help, you can always find a way through financially.

But as I write these words, there are hundreds, if not thousands, walking around in lower Manhattan today with pictures of loved ones, looking for those who will never be found.

This was an unscheduled pit stop for all of us. We have been permanently scarred by those four hijacked jets—scarred as a nation and scarred individually. And we'd better be ready for some changes.

This isn't what we envisaged, is it? Our dream was to work hard, raise our kids, invest wisely for retirement, climb the ladder, keep our health, and somewhere in our fifties retire to a beautiful home in the country or on a golf course to lead a quiet and fulfilling life.

But in this war, there are no safe places.

None.

Everything has officially changed. But that's nothing new. It happened to Robert E. Lee a long time ago. His long-term plans for a safe and quiet life were also interrupted. What's amazing is that his life was changed forever by a terrorist attack:

> Like many of us, Lee yearned for a quiet life. His constant wish was to farm an isolated piece of land in Virginia. That wish was never granted. But in the years before the War Between the States, Lee did inherit the responsibility for running the Arlington plantation, which was willed to his wife. His challenge was to do it successfully enough to pay off his father-in-law's debts and to finance the bequests he had willed to Lee's daughters. So Lee became a businessman."[6]

For the next two years, Lee poured himself into rebuilding the home where he and his wife had lived on and off for the last twenty years. It had lost its former glory, and Lee was consumed with the task of restoring its greatness. He was not repairing the past, but building for his family's future. But everything changed in one day. A surprise attack on a United States weapons facility would stun the entire country and change the plans of Robert E. Lee immediately.

J. Steven Wilkins fills us in:

The "insurrection" was, of course, the famous raid on Harper's Ferry by John Brown, the radical abolitionist and terrorist. He and his sons were fanatically devoted to the cause of abolitionism. He did not believe in non-violent opposition, however. Taking as his motto, "Without the shedding of blood there is no remission of sin" (Hebrews 9:22), Brown ignored the fact that the passage refers to Christ's sacrifice and instead determined to go on a murderous rampage to promote the crusade against slavery. Financed by six wealthy Unitarians (who do not believe that Jesus Christ is God), he had already made six bloody raids in Kansas. His targets were not always slave owners; indeed, the first victims of Brown's madness had been non-slaveholders who Brown had killed in cold blood, dragging them from their beds in the middle of the night. His purpose was not to bring vengeance but to promote terror. Now he had come to the South to provoke what he hoped would be a bloody slave rebellion. Early on Sunday morning, October 16, 1859, Brown led a small contingent of twenty-one men—sixteen white and five black—into Harper's Ferry to capture the Federal Arsenal."[7]

John Brown and his followers took hostages with them into the Federal Armory, including Lewis W. Washington, the grandnephew of President George Washington. This act of terrorism shocked the nation. And Robert E. Lee (who was on military leave), was called from his beloved Arlington to deal with the shocking assault. Under his command, the arsenal was attacked, retaken, and none of the hostages were harmed.

Lee's life, however, would never be the same after this terrorist attack. He had been on a leave of absence from the United States military to get his family affairs in order and the family farm back in repair. Then, he planned on returning to active duty, hoping to advance as an officer in the United States Army. The violent attack at Harper's Ferry, however, underscored the issue that split America. Events began to happen very quickly.

Abraham Lincoln, an outsider who was considered just a regional candidate for president, was elected by just 40 percent of the popular vote. Lincoln had been considered such a long shot that his name didn't even appear on the ballot in ten Southern states. He was definitely not the choice of the majority, but he was the winner.[8]

The election of Lincoln proved to be the last straw for the South. On December 20, 1860, South Carolina seceded from the Union. That was the first domino to fall. Mississippi, Florida, Alabama, Georgia, Louisiana, and Texas followed suit the following year.

Lee was opposed to secession at first. But he was also deeply concerned about states' rights. And then came the biggest career decision he would ever make. On April 18, 1861, through an intermediary by the name of Francis Preston Blair, President Abraham Lincoln offered to Robert E. Lee the command of the United States Army.

Here was the opportunity of a lifetime. Lee was offered command of an army of almost 100,000 men, with the full support of the government and the assistance of some of the ablest military men in the country, plus the rank of major-general. It was enough to make even the most principled of men to waver. But Lee apparently never hesitated. He later wrote, "After listening to his remarks, I declined the offer he made to me, to take command of the army that was to be brought into the field; stating, as candidly and courteously as I could, that, although opposed to secession and deprecating war, I could take no part in an invasion of the Southern States."[9]

And what was behind his reasoning? Lee was a Virginian. And interestingly enough, on the same day that Lee was offered the command of the United States Army, April 18, 1861, Virginia voted to secede from the Union. There was no way he could lead men into battle against his home state.

To understand Lee's convictions at this time, it is important to know that he believed quite clearly that his first allegiance was not to the nation but to his state. Prior to the war, it was commonplace for individuals to regard themselves first as citizens of their particular states, and only secondarily as citizens of the United States. For most, your state *was* your "country."[10]

We must understand the times to understand the man. Robert E. Lee walked away from the greatest career opportunity of his life as a matter of principle. Yes, he made the decision, but that doesn't take away from the fact that his plans, hopes, and dreams were permanently dashed by the tragic circumstances of an unwanted war.

His long-term dreams for the family plantation at Arlington were interrupted forever. He would never have the opportunity to enjoy the fruit of his hard work and diligent planning.

He never returned again to Arlington. As you know, Lee resigned from the United States Army and assumed command of the Confederate Army. His beloved home, Arlington, was confiscated by the federal government in 1864. The fields which Lee had so carefully cultivated with wheat and corn became a national cemetery sprouting thousands of white crosses.

Robert E. Lee, like you and me, had hopes and dreams for his career and family. But those plans were shattered by a terrorist attack masterminded by a crazed and half-insane religious zealot.

Lee had to turn down the opportunity of a lifetime. He had to die to the dreams of his heart and career for the greater good. And so too will some of us.

King David experienced the same kind of career interruption. Tragically, the enemy who tried to bring down his career was his own son, Absalom. Both Moses and Joshua experienced severe career interruptions, as did Joseph, Daniel, Paul, and the rest of the apostles.

Just about every man experiences the shell shock of a career interruption at some point in his life. And that leads us to the seven principles of Psalm 75 explained in the following pages. But before we head for the next chapter, I'd like to address one final thought.

When your career is interrupted, you're forced to wait. Most of us have no interest in waiting—for *anything*. Especially when it comes to our dreams and plans for our careers. We're movers and shakers. We've spent years developing our networks and polishing our résumés. We know how to make things happen. And we admire those who get around any and every obstacle that stands in the way of their dreams.

Jim Clark is a Silicon Valley legend. He's the only man to ever start three separate companies and take their company stock to the billion dollar mark. Just doing it once makes you a legend. But doing it three times qualifies you for sainthood in the technological Vatican that runs straight south down the I-280 spine of the San Francisco peninsula.

Years ago, Clark built a magnificent home in the gorgeous and secluded little town known as Atherton. The Clark mansion was surrounded by hills and beautiful countryside. But as the years went by and stock valuations soared in the valley, more and more millionaires began moving into the neighborhood. Houses—even bigger than Clark's—began to spring up on all sides. One morning he looked up from his morning coffee to look directly into the face of his neighbor as he sat on his home's adjoining deck. That was unacceptable to Jim Clark. So he filed for a building permit to build a higher fence around the perimeter of his property. The planning commission turned down his request, citing that fence could only be a certain height in the town. Clark's fence was already at the maximum height allowed.

Clark thought about his options. Within days, an armada of dump trucks began rumbling toward Clark's estate.

He didn't build a new fence.

He just built *a hill*.

There were no laws in Atherton against building hills. No one ever thought of building a hill. But when you're worth a billion or two, a hill is an option. And Clark built one. And then he stuck his original fence on top of the hill.

None of us like waiting for anything. But when God hems us in and makes us wait, He is worth waiting for. You may not have the money to build your own hill to speed up the process, but you serve a God who responds to faith by moving mountains.

And that's something worth waiting for.

SIX

CAREER INTERRUPTIONS

PART 2

The harder you work, the harder it is to surrender.

VINCE LOMBARDI

HOW IN THE WORLD CAN A KING GET LAID OFF?

Well, it happens. And it was one of the deepest pits of David's entire life.

If anyone knew the pit, it was David. But when his son Absalom sprung a trap to steal the throne from his father, it was a dagger into the deepest part of David's heart. David knew the pit and he knew it well. But there is no pit deeper than betrayal by your own boy.

A coup, a rebellion, took place right under David's nose. David never suspected it and never saw it coming. If you'd told him what was happening, he wouldn't have believed you.

For years, the betrayer in his court had set the stage to bring down David and take his place on the throne. Tragically, it was his son, Absalom, who overthrew him and drove him from the throne for a brief time. This was his own son! He loved this boy and gave him everything. It's one of the saddest stories in all of Scripture, and you can read all about it in 2 Samuel, chapters 15 through 20.

David knew what it was to be promoted and he knew what it was to be laid off. He even knew what it was to make a lateral career move. That's essentially what he did when he had to flee Jerusalem. Technically, he was still king. But he had to make a lateral move out of Jerusalem to stay alive and survive.

Most men in their lifetimes will experience something similar. At some point a promotion will come our way, but promotions aren't forever. A promotion is never permanent. Wasn't it Lou Holtz who said there are two kinds of coaches? Those who have been fired and those who will be.

Ultimately, God is behind *every* career move that you experience, whether it is up the ladder or down through the trapdoor into the recesses of the pit.

That's the message of Psalm 75:

For neither from the east nor from the west nor from the desert does
　promotion come;
But God is the Judge. He puts down one and promotes another. (vv.
　6–7, MLB)

Psalm 75 is the bottom line when it comes to promotion, layoffs, and plateauing. This psalm gives you insight that you'll never find from any head hunter or career counselor. In the final analysis:

- It is God who promotes.
- It is God who demotes.
- It is God who allows our careers to plateau.

In other words, God is completely in charge of your career. There is a divine side to your career and there is a human side. The human side is your network, your résumé, and your past achievements. The divine side is the unseen hand of God, accomplishing and bringing about His purpose through every circumstance of your life. Proverbs 16:9 sums it up nicely: "The mind of man plans his way, but the LORD directs his steps."

Proverbs 16:9 and Psalm 75:6–7, along with some of the previous texts we've already discussed, seem to yield at least six principles for a man and his career.

1. Ultimately, all promotion is from the Lord.
2. When God is ready to promote you, no person, no group, no superior, no human network can stand in His way.
3. Ultimately, all layoffs are from the Lord.
4. When God is ready to lay you off, no person, no group, no superior, no human network can stand in His way.
5. God will test you before He promotes you.
6. God will lay you off to test you.

David's career interruption lasted for a matter of weeks. In the economic downturn that we find ourselves in since our national war against terrorism began, your layoff may last longer than that. I hate to be the bearer of bad news, but that is reality. That's why I would like to turn to someone who experienced a much longer career interruption than David.

The man I have in mind is Joshua.

When Moses, the legendary leader of Israel died, it was Joshua who was appointed by God to succeed him. What a huge responsibility!

Jack Welch, legendary leader of General Electric for twenty years, is widely considered to be the best CEO in America. His innovative and fearless leadership is admired far and wide. As you might imagine, his shoes would not be easy ones to step into. Jeffrey Immelt was chosen to be Welch's successor. Immelt recently reflected on his first week of replacing a legend:

"I was chairman for two days, and then I had jets with my engines hit a building that I insured, which was covered by a network I owned...."[1]

Immelt took the reins during the very week that America found itself in its biggest crisis since the attack on Pearl Harbor. And he was expected to handle it just as the legendary Jack Welch would have done.

That's what Joshua faced. Talk about stepping into the sandals of a legend! To follow in the footsteps of Moses was no small matter. So God worked overtime to get Joshua ready, years and years before he would face that ultimate test.

And how was he tested?

By a major career interruption.

A Tale of Two Elevators

Moses wasn't a king, but at one point in his life he had been in line to possibly succeed the Pharaoh of Egypt. Then, at the age of forty, at the pinnacle of his career, and at the top of his game, a trapdoor opened beneath his feet, sending him tumbling into a *very* deep pit.

You might say Moses was laid off. And that layoff was such a shattering experience that Moses literally headed for the wilderness to a life of obscurity and apparent insignificance for the next forty years. But then one day he got a promotion, and wound up leading Israel for the next forty years. And when Moses died, Joshua was promoted.

Joshua had a completely different background from Moses. As you may recall, Moses had a shattering experience at the age of forty that took him another four decades to get over. Joshua didn't have to face a similar, traumatic situation.

Interestingly enough, Joshua had a period of time, like Moses, where he was in the wilderness. Like Moses, his period in the desert was also forty years in duration. And although they both endured the desert for forty years, their circumstances in the desert were very different.

I think the best way to explain the difference is to imagine two men on two separate elevators in the same skyscraper: Moses and Joshua. Moses occupies one elevator and Joshua the other. Both step into their elevators on the ground floor and push the buttons to rise over one hundred stories to get to the observation deck. From the observation deck, they can look over into the Promised Land.

The ride to the top proceeds nicely. Swift and smooth. Then, without warning, the cable in Moses' elevator snaps and his elevator car drops like a stone to the unrelenting basement below.

Moses survives the plunge, but he's in a state of shock as he looks around him. He finds himself in the twisted wreckage of very unfamiliar and unwelcome territory. And it will take him forty years to be free of the mangled and contorted circumstances of that time in his life. When you look at the life of Moses, there is no question that for him, the bottom literally dropped out. Talk about an unscheduled pit stop!

Over in the other elevator, Joshua cruises toward the observation deck and that panoramic view of the Promised Land. There's no alarm, no jolt, no swaying. The elevator has simply ground to a halt. Joshua finds himself stuck somewhere between the fortieth and forty-first floor. And believe it or not, he will remain stuck between floors for *forty years.*

It took Joshua four, long decades to get out of that stinking, confining box suspended hundreds of feet above the earth. When you look at the life of Joshua, you will find that the bottom never did drop out. He just got stuck between floors. Or to put it another way, he *plateaued.* For forty years he didn't go up and he didn't go down, he just stayed exactly the same.

THE LONG PLATEAU

Not everyone has the bottom drop out. Some people just plateau. But both elevators are controlled by the same omnipotent and omniscient Operator, and each elevator contains its own lessons. The point is this: both Moses and Joshua were promoted by God to the top spot in Israel. But before they could be promoted they were both prepared.

God prepared one by letting the bottom drop out. He prepared the other by letting him plateau. What they had in common was this: before they were promoted in their careers, their careers were significantly interrupted.

Moses crashed and spent forty years crawling out of the wreckage.

Joshua was put on hold and waited for forty years.

And God was in charge the entire time.

Have you been laid off in the recent economic crunch? In His time, God will put you back to work. But for now, you're on hold. You've plateaued. Plateauing is an interesting concept. You can plateau because you're out of a job and you can plateau even *in* a job. Neither experience is one that a man relishes. But the lessons are priceless.

Career plateauing is becoming a national phenomenon. A case could be made that it is the number one career dilemma in America. For years, it has been the experience of many professionals to receive promotions every two to three years. But things are changing. It's now more like five to seven years before a promotion comes down the line—if it comes at all. Corporations are cutting back. And now, with America in an ongoing war with an invisible enemy in our midst, there will be more cutbacks than ever.

The idea of languishing on a plateau is tough to handle when your entire mind-set is geared to motoring up the slopes. When you're plateaued, you can't get it in gear. You're stuck in neutral. Or, to go back to the original metaphor, you're stuck between floors.

One reason it's so tough to be plateaued is because we treasure such high expectations of continual advancement. For nearly a generation promotion has been a "gimme" for those who worked hard. But as Bob Dylan used to sing, "The Times, They Are A-Changin'." Things today are almost the reverse of what they were. When executives with Ivy League MBAs and fifteen years' experience and high six-figure incomes are plateauing (and happy to still have a job), then it doesn't take rocket science to figure out that promotions are going to be few and far between for everyone else on the corporate ladder.

There's a big difference between plateauing and hitting bottom. There is a difference between a mid-life crisis and a mid-life plateau. The guy who bottoms out in mid-life is the guy who leaves his wife and kids, buys a red Corvette, several feet of gold chains, and applies Rogaine to his bald spots three time a day.

The guy who plateaus in mid-life doesn't do that. He still loves his wife and kids, he keeps his SUV, the only chain he owns is in the backyard in a chain link fence, and spending money for Rogaine isn't on his budgetary priority list.

Not everyone winds up with an experience like Moses'. Joshua didn't, and he was Moses' successor. Joshua struggled with something else: He may have been the very first guy to go through career plateauing. Yes, he was eventually promoted to the next spot. But it was quite a wait between promotions. About forty-year's worth.

GOD WILL TEST YOU BEFORE HE PROMOTES YOU

Moses didn't start out as the leader of Israel, and neither did Joshua. That's because God's method is to test a man before He uses a man. It was true of Joseph, it was true of David, it was true of Daniel, and it was true of Paul. In God's administration, preparation always precedes promotion. God will teach the man and then He will test the man.

You may be thinking, "Wait a minute. Didn't we already discuss this testing stuff? Why are we going over it again? I need a job, not more stuff on testing. I just need to get a job and get out of this pit."

I understand why you might feel that way. The financial pressure on a man with a family is enormous. Of course you're interested in getting back to work or finding a more meaningful kind of work. God understands that completely. But there is more at stake here than the fact that you are plateaued. God is using your plateau situation to accomplish some other objectives in your life.

He will see you through. He will get you through this. He will bring you out of that pit. But don't forget that He wants to make you a better man. You want a job. He wants more for you than that. It was F. B. Meyer who observed, "God's greatest gifts to man come through travail. Whether we look into the spiritual or temporal sphere, can we discover anything, any great reform, any beneficial discovery, any soul-waking revival, which did not come through toil and tears, the vigils and blood-shedding of men and women whose suffering were the pangs of its birth?"[2]

There is an age-old debate about leadership. Are leaders born or are leaders made? To begin with, every leader I have ever met, by necessity, had to be born. So yes, leaders are born.

But are leaders *made?* When it comes to spiritual leadership, the answer is yes. To be more precise, God makes His leaders by *refining*—as steel is refined in the searing heat of the blast furnace. God's leaders for ministry, business, home, academics, and every field of expertise are refined. They are refined through the process of testing.

So here we are back to testing. Losing a job is a test. Waiting for a job is a test. Plateauing in a job is a test. Yes, this is a test.

There are at least three ways that God will test a person that He desires to use. I'm going to enumerate just three, but undoubtedly there are others. I mention these three because you find them so often in the lives of spiritual leaders—past and present. I think it's safe to say that almost any spiritual leader you know of who is being used by God has been through some form of these three tests. And what is it that God tests? Primarily, He tests a man's character.

This brings us to a very critical principle that every leader and potential leader must know: *Character development comes before ministry.* That's why

God will take the time to test you. It doesn't matter if you're an accountant, a body and fender man, a professional athlete, a professor, a middle-school teacher, an entrepreneur, a pastor, an engineer, or a sales manager. God desires for His people in all walks of life to be His ministers right where they are. But you can count on this: He will test you before He will use you. Now let's look at the three tests.

THE TEST OF STANDING ALONE

Do the names Shammua, Shaphat, Igal, Palti, Gaddiel, Gaddi, Ammiel, Sethur, Nahbi, and Geuel ring a bell? No, they're not a law firm in New Jersey. But these ten guys did have something significant in common: They were all chicken.

Moses had given twelve men an assignment: They were to run a reconnaissance mission into Canaan and check out the situation before the nation crossed over to occupy the land.

When General Norman Schwarzkopf gave his now famous briefing at the end of the Gulf War, he briefly mentioned the special forces that went into Kuwait and Iraq to take a look at things firsthand before the land campaign took place. They went in to be Schwarzkopf's eyes and ears behind enemy lines. And that was the precise mission of the dozen guys who slipped into Canaan. The whole scenario is recorded in Numbers 13.

> When Moses sent them to spy out the land of Canaan, he said to them, "Go up there into the Negev; then go up into the hill country. See what the land is like, and whether the people who live in it are strong or weak, whether they are few or many. How is the land in which they live, is it good or bad? And how are the cities in which they live, are they like open camps or with fortifications? How is the land, is it fat or lean? Are there trees in it or not? Make an effort then to get some of the fruit of the land." (vv. 17–20)

This Israeli reconnaissance team went into Canaan for forty days to find out the answers to Moses' questions. After forty days they returned to General Moses with their report.

When they returned from spying out the land, at the end of forty days, they proceeded to come to Moses and Aaron and to all the congregation of the sons of Israel in the wilderness of Paran, at Kadesh; and they brought back word to them and to all the congregation and showed them the fruit of the land. Thus they told him, and said, "We went in to the land where you sent us; and it certainly does flow with milk and honey, and this is its fruit. Nevertheless, the people who live in the land are strong, and the cities are fortified and very large; and moreover, we saw the descendants of Anak there. Amalek is living in the land of the Negev and the Hittites and the Jebusites and the Amorites are living in the hill country, and the Canaanites are living by the sea and by the side of the Jordan." (vv. 25–29)

Ten out of the twelve gave a report that was at best pessimistic. They were like the guy who said, "I was going to read a book on positive thinking, and then I thought: *What good would that do?*" Obviously, these guys had never read Norman Vincent Peale—or Robert Schuller, either. But positive thinking wasn't the issue here. The issue was faith in God and what He had promised to do. Caleb and Joshua were the lone voices of optimism, and they were optimistic because they believed in the power of God. But those ten other Special Operations guys panicked. Caleb tried to get the floor, but he could barely finish a sentence before being interrupted by these ten crybabies.

But the men who had gone up with him said, "We are not able to go up against the people, for they are too strong for us." So they gave out to the sons of Israel a bad report of the land which they had spied out, saying, "The land through which we have gone, in spying it out, is a land that devours its inhabitants; and all the people whom we saw in it are men of great size. There also we saw the Nephilim (the sons of Anak are part of the Nephilim); and we became like grasshoppers in our own sight, and so we were in their sight." (vv. 31–33)

These references to the sons of Anak and the Nephilim don't mean much to us, but they obviously meant a lot to the ten hens. The Anakites and the

Nephilim were literal giants—people of tremendous size and strength. When the ten saw them, they felt like grasshoppers. That last line of verse 33 is significant. Because the ten felt like grasshoppers in their own hearts, that's exactly how they were perceived. They were beaten before they ever got started.

Joshua and Caleb had another perspective. And they stood squarely against the weak and feeble report of the ten. But panic is more contagious than a cold virus in a church nursery. And within moments of the bad report, the entire camp was infected.

> Then all the congregation lifted up their voices and cried, and the people wept that night. All the sons of Israel grumbled against Moses and Aaron; and the whole congregation said to them, "Would that we had died in the land of Egypt! Or would that we had died in this wilderness! Why is the LORD bringing us into this land, to fall by the sword? Our wives and our little ones will become plunder; would it not be better for us to return to Egypt?" So they said to one another, "Let us appoint a leader and return to Egypt."
>
> Then Moses and Aaron fell on their faces in the presence of all the assembly of the congregation of the sons of Israel. Joshua the son of Nun and Caleb the son of Jephunneh, of those who had spied out the land, tore their clothes; and they spoke to all the congregation of the sons of Israel, saying, "The land which we passed through to spy out is an exceedingly good land. If the LORD is pleased with us, then He will bring us into this land and give it to us a land which flows with milk and honey. Only do not rebel against the LORD; and do not fear the people of the land, for they will be our prey. Their protection has been removed from them, and the LORD is with us; do not fear them." But all the congregation said to stone them with stones. Then the glory of the LORD appeared in the tent of meeting to all the sons of Israel. (Numbers 14:1–10)

This was Joshua's time of testing. He had to learn to stand alone. But wait. It's pretty clear that Joshua *and* Caleb stood against the ten. So Joshua really wasn't alone.

I would like to suggest that Joshua did stand alone. I would also like to suggest that Caleb stood alone. I think it's clear that Joshua would have stood without Caleb—and that Caleb would have stood without Joshua. So in essence, both Joshua and Caleb stood alone. They just happened to stand alone together.

This was a pretty heated situation. I've been in some tense congregational meetings before, but this one was a doozy. Caleb and Joshua simply weren't wired to "go along to get along." They refused to bow their knees to the idols of popularity and expediency. They stood on the truth and they were not going to move.

Why does God test this aspect of a man before God will use him? Because God's men must be willing to listen to God and to obey Him regardless of how unpopular it may make them. God's men are not politicians who rely on focus groups or take a poll to determine what position they should take on a given issue.

This is why God's men must be different. They must lead from the power of their lives rather than out of a carefully crafted synthetic integrity put together by a public relations firm.

God's men stand for the truth when no one else is standing for it. Peter Marshall once prayed, "Dear Lord, give us clear vision that we may know where to stand and what to stand for, because unless we stand for something, we shall fall for anything."

God's men cannot be men who strive for popularity. For God's way is rarely popular. God is looking for men who can stand in the furnace and take the heat. You may be the only guy in your company who doesn't pad his expense account. If that's the case, you won't be popular. You'll get some heat from all of the rest. But the question is this: Can you stand alone? Perhaps your boss insists that you lie in order to edge out the competition and close the deal. Can you stand alone and take the heat?

Let me ask you a question: When was the last time you stood alone?

There is a reason that God tests us to see if we can stand alone. In fact there are a couple. Standing alone is a process that God uses to

- check your obedience
- check your integrity

When God calls a man to stand alone, He is specifically checking a man's obedience in the fires of adversity and his integrity in the pull and tug of a generation that thrives on moral compromise. Some men pass the test. Others don't. It's the rare man in our society who does pass the test. John Gardner comments:

In recent years we have been puzzled by a steady parade of intelligent, successful Americans who have destroyed their own careers through amoral or criminal acts—from ambitious public servants to greedy Wall Street figures. Gifted and richly rewarded, they overreached and brought themselves crashing down. A common assumption is that for a price (money, power, fame, sensual pleasure) they betrayed their standards. The other possibility is that they did not have any standards to betray, that they were among the many contemporary individuals who had roots in no set of values, or have torn loose from their roots. A society afflicted with the disintegration of family and community will inevitably feed such gifted transgressors into the stream of our national life."[3]

Reputation is what people think you are. Character is what you are when no one else is around. That's why God tests character. Moses passed this test and so did Joshua and Caleb. But Saul failed the test of standing alone. He failed it several times. In the clutch, Saul did not have obedience and he did not have integrity. That's why God couldn't use him. Saul was a guy who was always taking the easy way out. If everyone else was doing it, he would do it. If God wanted him to do something one way, Saul thought another way was better. Saul was a failure because he developed a habit of taking moral shortcuts. That's why he failed the test. And his leadership mark in Israel barely warranted an asterisk.

Charles Colson's words are appropriate here:

In my extensive travels over the past twelve years, I've met with pastors, talked with church members, and spoken in hundreds of churches. And from my observations I must conclude that the church, broadly speaking, has succumbed to many of the culture's enticements.

I don't want to generalize or be overly harsh, but it's fair to say that much of the church is caught up in the success mania of American society. Often more concerned with budgets and building programs than with the body of Christ, the church places more emphasis on growth than repentance. Suffering, sacrifice, and service has been preempted by success and self-fulfillment.

One pastor confided to me, "I try not to talk about subjects that make people uncomfortable. My job is to make sure they come back here week after week."[4]

Somewhere along the line, that pastor misread his biblical job description. His job is to please Christ, and, when necessary, to stand alone. That's it. Here's the thing about standing alone: It all comes down to who you're trying to please. Are you trying to please a congregation, a board, some powerful person in the denomination, an executive vice president in your company, or a well-connected person in your profession? Or are you trying to please Christ? You can't please both. And the only one who ultimately matters is Christ.

Are you a people pleaser or a Christ pleaser? That's the bottom line when it comes to standing alone.

In your time of plateauing, don't go it alone. Look for a Caleb with whom you can "stand alone together." Look for a guy who would stand alone even if you don't. And you be that kind of man as well.

And when you write up your résumé or go to an interview, tell the truth. Don't hedge the truth and don't pad the facts. You don't have to do that to gain employment. God is your employer. And He is watching to see what you will do under the pressure of a prolonged pit.

THE TEST OF DEEP DISAPPOINTMENT

Needless to say, the ten spies miserably failed their test. Not only did they doubt the power of God, but they virtually incited a mob scene by their contagious unbelief. As a result, God moved in devastating judgment against the whole nation.

We never sin alone. Our sin always brings consequences into the lives of others. When I personally sin, I must live with the consequences, but so must others. This is what happened to Joshua and Caleb. Though they had been faithful, they had to tread sand for forty years before they were allowed to enter the Promised Land. That had to be a crushing disappointment. It would have been one thing if they'd been disobedient. But they hadn't! They had been obedient. They had done everything right. They had argued passionately for God's plan and God's timing.

If God is going to develop your character, at some point you will come face-to-face with deep disappointment. And it will be deeper than you ever imagined. Why was Joshua plateaued between floors for forty years? Because of his sin? No, it was because of someone else's sin.

This situation was pregnant with significance. This test of deep disappointment was a very critical test, for it would have been very easy for Joshua and Caleb to allow bitterness and resentment to get the best of them. They could have wallowed every day in a new pond of inviting and indulgent self-pity. That would have been the easy thing to do. And it would have soured their spirits and disqualified Joshua from his intended leadership position.

Every morning for forty years, Joshua woke up and had to make a decision. Would he live that day in bitterness or resentment, or would he trust God with his life?

Sportscaster Harry Kalas once introduced Philadelphia Phillies outfielder Garry Maddox with the following words: "Garry has turned his life around. He used to be depressed and miserable. Now he's miserable and depressed."[5]

How about you? Are you bitter and resentful? Or are you resentful and bitter? Perhaps you've been deeply disappointed by someone close to you. It may have been a brother, a trusted friend, or a spouse. Those are the deepest disappointments of all. Those kinds of broken trusts have the greatest potential of releasing the twin toxins of bitterness and resentment into your soul.

I can't help but think of the story of one Leonard Holt. This guy had been a paragon of respectability in his community. He was a middle-aged, hardworking lab technician who had been employed at the same

Pennsylvania paper mill for nineteen years. Having been a Boy Scout leader, an affectionate father, a member of the local fire brigade, and a regular church attender, he was admired as a model in his community. Until the day he snapped.

On one very carefully planned day, Leonard Holt, a proficient marksman, concealed two pistols in his coat pockets and drove to the mill where he had worked for so many years. Wordlessly, he walked slowly into his shop and began firing with calculated frenzy. He killed several co-workers with two or three bullets apiece, firing more than thirty shots, cutting down men he had known for more than fifteen years. People were shocked that Leonard was the killer. It just didn't make sense.

Puzzled police investigators finally found a train of logic behind his brief reign of terror. Down deep within the heart of Leonard Holt, resentment rumbled and seethed like trapped magma. His monk-like exterior concealed the churning hatred within. The investigation yielded the following facts. Several victims had been promoted over him while he remained in the same position. Leonard Holt was eaten alive by his bitterness and resentment, and his rage finally came gushing to the surface. Beneath his picture in *Time* magazine, the caption told the story: "Responsible, Respectable, and Resentful."[6]

Leonard Holt was stuck between floors. And it ate him alive. He allowed his disappointment to master his life. It was William H. Walton who once observed that "to carry a grudge is like being stung to death by one bee."

After the Civil War, Robert E. Lee visited the beautiful home of a wealthy Kentucky widow. After a charming lunch she invited him to join her on the porch. She then pointed to a once majestic magnolia tree that had been badly burned and charred by Northern artillery fire. The woman began to cry as she described the former magnificence of the once stately tree that had shaded the family house for generations. Through tear-laden lashes she looked to General Lee for a word condemning the North—or at least to sympathize with her loss.

After pausing for several seconds, Lee said, "My dear madam, cut it down and forget it."

The only way to cut down the deep roots of bitterness and resentment that spring from deep disappointment is to redirect your focus toward God.

No one portrayed that attitude better than Joseph, son of Jacob. Confronting his terrified brothers, who years before had sold him to slave traders, he said "You meant evil against me, but God meant it for good in order to bring about this present result" (Genesis 50:20).

Joseph, in time, was able to see an explanation for the deep disappointment of his life. But long before he ever got an explanation, he had to cut down the bitterness and resentment. So did Joshua and Caleb. And so do you.

In the midst of this look at the test of deep disappointment, it's easy to forget something that is notable: Joshua *passed* this test. And though promotion was a long time coming, he was ultimately promoted.

THE TEST OF TRUSTING GOD'S TIMING

God's timing is always impeccable.

We have great difficulty at times understanding God's timing. It doesn't make sense to us. In fact, from our perspective, He isn't even close to being on schedule. I'm sure that Joshua had his struggles with God's timing. Joshua had to wrestle with God's timing for forty years. Through the very prime of his life, Joshua was plateaued in a dreary wilderness. And life was passing him by every day. God's timing can be enormously difficult to understand.

When Sally O'Malley of County Clare won the Irish Sweepstakes, she decided to treat herself to some of the finer things in life. "I've nivver had a milk bath," she told her milkman one morning. "Wouldja be bringin' me 96 quarts o'milk tomorrow?"

"Whattiver ye want, mum," answered the milkman. "Will that be pasturized?"

"No," said she. "Up to me chest will do."

Sometimes it is extremely difficult to understand another person. It is virtually impossible to understand the timing of God before it takes place. And sometimes you won't even understand it when it does take place. God tells us in Scripture that we will occasionally have a hard time with His methods. As we noted in an earlier chapter, He tells us this right up front:

"My thoughts are not your thoughts,
Neither are your ways My ways," declares the LORD.

"For as the heavens are higher than the earth,
So are My ways higher than your ways
And My thoughts than your thoughts." (Isaiah 55:8–9)

When it comes to the issue of timing, we shouldn't be surprised that His ways are not our ways. Yet we are. When it comes to the issue of timing, we shouldn't be surprised that His thoughts don't line up with our thoughts. God thinks differently about timing than we do. That's why His time is not our time.

I'm sure at times that Joshua must have thought life was passing right by him. Maybe you're having the same thoughts of late. But God's thoughts aren't your thoughts. God has thought about something else that you cannot see. The fact of the matter is this. When you are plateaued, you may think that life is passing you by, but it isn't. Your life is in His hand. And He knows precisely what He is doing with your life. If you stay faithful, at the right time He will reward your faithfulness.

Waiting for His timing is tough. You will struggle with His timing, and at other times you will fight His timing. But that's okay. It's just part of the process as you learn to accept the control of the One whose thoughts are not your thoughts.

A young boy carried the cocoon of a moth into his house to watch the fascinating events that would take place when the moth emerged. When the moth finally started to break out of his cocoon, the boy noticed how hard the moth had to struggle. The process was slow, exceedingly slow. In an effort to help, the boy reached down and widened the opening of the cocoon. Soon the moth was out of its prison.

But as the boy watched, the wings remained shriveled. Something was wrong. What the boy hadn't realized was that the struggle to get out of the cocoon was essential for the moth's muscle system to develop. In a misguided effort to relieve the struggle, the boy had crippled forever the future of the moth.[7]

God never allows the cocoon to open until the time is precisely right. You may be feeling that you will be plateaued forever. You may be discouraged because you have been stuck between floors longer than you ever thought possible. Don't lose heart. God is overseeing your struggle as you are caught between floors. Remain open and teachable, and at the right moment, He will do for you what He has done for so many others. He will provide a way of escape. And you will not only be free of your cocoon, but you will be fully developed and ready to fly.

Leonard Ravenhill tells about a group of tourists visiting a picturesque village who walked by an old man sitting beside a fence. In a rather patronizing way, one tourist asked, "Were any great men born in this village?"

The old man replied, "Nope, only babies."[8]

There is no such thing as instant greatness or instant maturity. We have instant oatmeal, instant coffee, instant soup, and microwave popcorn. Some people can't even imagine life without a microwave. We demand immediate gratification! But in the Christian life, there are no microwaves.

There are, however, Crock-Pots.

Crock-Pots are *slow* cookers. They need time, plenty of time. Spiritual maturity never comes in a package with microwave instructions. That's because spiritual maturity can only be produced in Crock-Pots. That's why God puts His leaders through the Crock-Pot. Joshua was in the Crock-Pot, Moses was in the Crock-Pot, Caleb was in the Crock-Pot, Joseph was in the Crock-Pot, and you may be in the Crock-Pot.

God puts His leaders in the very slowest of slow cookers, because when the time is right, they're not only done, but they're tender. And that's the kind of leader God can use. An effective spiritual leader needs a tender heart toward God. Tenderness can't happen in the microwave. That's why you're in the Crock-Pot.

Sometimes plateaued people wonder if God really loves them. They get so tired of waiting. May I let you in on a secret? God does love you. As a matter of fact, He loves you tender. And He will never let you go. Never. That's why you can trust His timing.

Our premise was this: God will test you before He promotes you. That simply means that God will work *in* you before He works *through* you. Then He can promote you.

A word of caution is in order here: Scripture contains no blanket promise that God will promote you. Some are promoted but others are not (see Hebrews 11:32–40). But there is a blanket promise that He will be faithful to you. And that's the most important thing. God will be faithful to do what is best for you. That's the promise of 2 Timothy 2:13: "If we are faithless, He remains faithful, for He cannot deny Himself."

There are two options when you are plateaued. One is to completely yield yourself to the Master's wisdom and timing. The other is to bolt and begin scheming to get what you so desperately want. There's nothing wrong with changing your circumstances if you can legitimately do so. Get those résumés out and make as many calls as you can. That's all legitimate and what you should be doing. But don't shortchange the truth in the process. Don't compromise your integrity. Warren Wiersbe is right: Faith is living without scheming. Remember, this is a test. Pass it.

He knows your situation. He sees you down in that pit. He knows your desire and understands your pressure. And He knows the right time to pull you out of that hole in the ground too. In the meantime, be faithful where you are. Be as faithful as you possibly can today, and trust Him for your future.

Be faithful in the pit.

Be faithful in the unscheduled pit stop.

Follow Him with all of your heart. Show Him your faithfulness in the place you don't want to be.

It was the Lord Jesus Christ who said, "He who is faithful in a very little thing is faithful also in much" (Luke 16:10).

No matter where your elevator ride through life takes you, He'll bring you out on the right floor, at the right time. Count on it.

SEVEN

TOTALED OUT

When I remember God, then I am disturbed.

PSALM 77: 3

I WAS ON THE PHONE LAST WEEK with a guy who was in deep yogurt.

He's in his early thirties, married, with a new baby. He's been out of work for nearly ten months and he's just about ready to go under.

As he told me his story, I made a comment.

"That sounds just like 1983."

"Why? What happened in 1983?"

"What you're going through," I explained, "sounds very similar to what I went through in '83. I'll never forget that year as long as I live. That may have been the toughest year of my life."

"*You* went through something like I'm going through?"

He sounded so shocked and incredulous I almost had to smile. So I leaned back in my chair and began to tell him about all that happened to me that year when I was in my early thirties, married, with two kids.

His response was classic. "I didn't know *you* had been through anything like that!"

So often, that's the way it is when we're in the pit. We feel all alone, and can't imagine that anyone has ever faced what we're facing in all our troubles and trials. I think this guy got off the phone actually feeling better about his situation, realizing that he wasn't the only man to ever go through something like that.

I've written about unscheduled pit stops because I've been there. I've written about the battle of all battles because, at one point in my life, I was right in the thick of it.

When you're battling to understand God, it helps to know that you're not the first to ever fight that fight. For that reason, I'm going to take the presumptuous step of telling you the story of what happened to me back in 1983. I've been in pits several times since that were just as deep. But I won't delve into those episodes right now.

1983 was my introduction to the pit.

1983 just about totaled me out.

And in a strange sort of way, the story may actually encourage you. The words of C. S. Lewis come to mind as I begin my story: "Think of me as a fellow-patient in the same hospital who, having been admitted a little earlier, could give some advice."

THE TOUGHEST CHAPTER

I love to browse in bookstores. I can literally spend hours perusing book after book. It usually doesn't take me long to find my way to the biography section. Before long, I'll be paging through new books on Lincoln, Stalin, Gandhi, Gehrig, Lindbergh, and Truman, just to name a few.

Most of us will never have books written about our lives. But I have a theory about that. Even though we may never have a biography written about us, our lives still contain "chapters." Most people can look back over their lives and see very clear chapters. It may be a two-year chapter in the military, a four-year chapter in high school, or a seven-year chapter living in a particular city.

Nearly twenty years ago, Mary and I entered into a chapter that proved to be, at least up until that point, the toughest of our lives. Tougher than I could have ever imagined. One morning I remember sitting in my car at an intersection, waiting for the light to change, and fighting with all my might to hold back the tears. I didn't know it at the time, but I was about one year into what would prove to be a three-year chapter.

What had transpired at the beginning of this new chapter? Allow me to back up a little bit and get a running start on the story. I'd been pastoring for four years. I started this first pastorate at the ripe old age of twenty-eight.

Fresh out of seminary, I knew just enough to be dangerous. But at the time I didn't know it. I imagined myself very capable, with tremendous potential for the future. I expected God to do some great things. And He did.

But after four years of working long hours, doing too much counseling, and not having the wisdom to pace myself, I found myself completely out of motivation and vision as to where the church should go next. Quite frankly, I was emotionally out of gas.

Years later I would read an article by Bill Hybels that graphically explained what I was experiencing. Hybels pointed out that every person needs to monitor three internal gauges: the physical, the spiritual, and the emotional. Hybels mentioned a particular crisis time in his own life. It caught him by surprise, because he'd been diligent to keep himself in physical and spiritual balance. What he hadn't realized was that there is another gauge—an emotional one. This particular gauge (if he'd known about it) would have given him an accurate reading of the level within his emotional tank. But he had no awareness of such a gauge. As a result, the emotional side of his life was never replenished.

When I heard him tell that story, I thought to myself, *That's exactly what happened to me!*

As a result, I found myself at a point where I was completely out of motivation. I couldn't manufacture it; I couldn't fake it; I couldn't understand it. My emotional engine had been running on fumes, but I hadn't realized it. I had no clue as to what was going on with me. All I knew was that I wasn't as motivated as I once was to shepherd the flock. As a result, I began making some poor decisions.

In my immaturity, I reasoned that what I needed was another challenge, another flock to shepherd. A new challenge in a new setting (I told myself) would get my juices flowing again. Surely that was the answer. After one year of struggling daily with insufficient motivation, and quite frankly, feeling guilty for taking money for a job I didn't think I was doing well, I decided to resign. It was the only solution that I could see.

There was only one problem. I didn't have a call to another ministry.

At the time, I honestly didn't see that "small detail" as a problem. I figured if God was leading me (and I was fairly sure that He was), then He would provide the next opportunity. That was my first mistake. Instead of waiting on the Shepherd to lead, I got ahead of the Shepherd—a very foolish thing to do.

I made my second mistake when I neglected to go after ample counsel before I made my decision. I talked to a few friends in ministry who were about my own age, but my mistake was in not talking to some other men who were much older and wiser than my peers. So there I was, thirty-three years old, stepping out in front of the Shepherd without mature advice or counsel. I now look back and wonder how I could have been so stupid.

So one Sunday morning I stepped up into the pulpit and announced my resignation. People were shocked. The church was growing, healthy, and people were coming to Christ and being discipled. Given that scenario, they couldn't understand why I was leaving. Especially when they realized I had nowhere else to go! Some even met with me, hoping to persuade me to change my mind. But my mind was made up.

I was even more convinced I'd made the right decision when, on the day after my resignation, I received a call from a church in another state to see if I would be willing to candidate for their senior pastor position. In my four years at the church, I'd never been contacted by another church. Then on the day after my resignation, another church called! What timing! I was right after all! God was leading. Everything was going to work out.

As my kids used to say, "Not!" But I didn't know it at the time.

I was ecstatic to have received this phone call. It was from a very well-known church in another state. Recently they had been through hard times and now they faced a challenging situation. But that's exactly what I needed: a new challenge.

Within just a couple of weeks, Mary and I flew out to meet with the search committee and to speak at the services on Sunday. Everything went great. When I was finished speaking on Sunday morning, the elders asked me if I might be available to speak the following Sunday! By the time we left several days later to go home, it looked like the church would extend a call for us to take the position. As we were flying back home, all we could see were green lights up ahead of us. Surely this was God's leading! I couldn't believe how well things were working out.

We expected the call to come right away. But one day went by, then two. Pretty soon a week had slipped past. We still hadn't heard anything. Then I received a call from a pastor friend of mine. He was calling to let me know he'd just received a call from that church to see if he would be interested in the position. They didn't know we were friends and that he knew I had also been under consideration. When he asked them about my status, they were a little taken aback. But they told him they'd decided not to extend a call to me. That's how I found out that I was out of the running.

The news rocked me back on my heels just a little. Everything had seemed to be on track. Our trip had gone so well, and they'd even asked me to stay over another Sunday. For the life of me, I couldn't figure what might have gone wrong. But I didn't have much time to puzzle over it. The very next afternoon I received a call from another search committee in another state wondering if I would be willing to consider their church. All right! So *that's* why the first situation didn't work out! God obviously had something else up His sleeve that I couldn't see. Things were beginning to come into focus now. I thought God wanted me at Church A, but now Church B was calling and seemed very, very interested.

Within a couple of weeks we made another trip, and once again things went well. There seemed to be a real interest on both sides and a mutual understanding. Our philosophies and ministry approaches seemed to fit hand-in-glove. All in all, it was a very positive time. All indications were that God was giving us a big thumbs-up. We returned home waiting for their follow-up call. One day, two days, three days, and then a week went by. But the call never came. Finally, after another week, I called them. They told me that it had been a very close vote, but they'd decided against pursuing me as a candidate.

I couldn't believe it. Once again, things had looked so positive. We seemed to have such a rapport. Needless to say, I was pretty discouraged when I went to bed that evening. But when I got up the next morning, guess what happened? Yep. Another church called.

I won't go into details except to say that this third prospect excited me even more than the first two. Evidently, this was why the first two didn't work out! God was saying no to those two because He had something much better in mind for me. And it looked like this was really it. Once again I got on a plane and made the trek to talk with the search committee. Once again it looked like a green light. But at the last moment (you guessed it) it all fell apart.

I was now 3 for 3. Or maybe I should say 0 for 3. What's hard to believe now, as I look back on those days, is that the same scenario happened *four more times*. That's right. Just several months later I found myself 0 for 7. Seven churches in a row had contacted me, met with me, listened to me preach, and then turned me down. And somewhere along the line I began taking those rejections personally. Most men get their self-worth from what they do, and I wasn't doing anything! So for the first time in my life, I started to deal with waves of depression.

I'd never dealt with such feelings before. At least not like that. Like everyone else, I'd had a few "down" days now and then. But this was more than being down; this was much more serious stuff. And I didn't have a clue as to how I should deal with it.

I should mention here that, up until this point, I had never really understood people who were dealing with depression. I can remember walking into Christian bookstores, seeing those rows of books on depression, and silently smirking to myself, *What's with all this depression stuff?* About the only time I ever struggled with depression was after preaching a poor sermon on Sunday. But then I'd watch Monday-night football and snap out of it. No wonder I didn't have much compassion for those in the grip of depression. I had absolutely no idea what they were going through.

But I was about to find out.

PILING ON

Did I mention that during this time Mary had two surgeries? Just several days after Mary had gone to Atlanta to visit her folks, I got a call one morning from her dad. He told me that he was at the hospital with Mary. She had wakened that morning with her leg swollen to almost twice its normal size. He had rushed her to the hospital where the doctor diagnosed the problem as phlebitis.

Apparently a blood clot had formed several days prior when Mary sprained her ankle. That injury, combined with holding a baby in her lap for five hours in a pressurized cabin, had been the catalyst for creating the clot. By the time Mary got to the hospital, the clot had gone from the ankle to her abdomen, where it had stabilized. Apparently, it was on its way to her heart.

When Carl told me this over the phone, I really wasn't shocked. It all seemed to fit in with everything else that was going wrong in our lives over the previous six to eight months. But I still had a little bit of hope. There was a church that really wanted us to come. In fact, there were two of them. But one in particular seemed to have the most promise. This most recent development with Mary caused me to make up my mind. Although I had some reservations, I was going to take that church!

My reasoning process was simple. They had offered us a very good salary, and we hadn't received a paycheck for nearly eight months (except for the money I made between Thanksgiving and Christmas driving a delivery truck for minimum wage). They had also very graciously offered to replace Mary's car that we'd had to sell. Here I was, nine months out of ministry, nine months out of money, with a wife in the hospital and two kids to take care of with a fresh stack of hospital bills.

When I talked to Mary that night, I told her I was coming to Atlanta, but that I was going to first fly to this other city to meet with the church board to accept their invitation and work out the remaining details. She said that she felt good about the church and the people (we had visited with them for several days the previous month) and that she felt right about us accepting their invitation.

All right! We were finally going to get the Farrar show back on the road. I actually had a church that had said, "Yes!" I was going to get down there and sign on the dotted line before they changed their minds.

I've got good new and bad news. The good news is that they didn't change their minds. The bad news is that I did. What in the world went wrong? It's actually pretty simple.

I got into that meeting and looked into the excited, expectant faces of those board members. But instead of sharing their excitement, I felt like I had a big rock in my gut. I had an overwhelming, unshakable sense that I was about to make a very large mistake. I was already in hot water, but taking a church just because it would solve our financial woes was just asking for boiling water. As I sat there with those men, I realized I was not their man—even though I wished that I was. But in my spirit, I knew it would be disobedient to say yes. So I said no.

For once someone other than me was shocked. They thought it was a done deal, and I said no. I thought about that for a few minutes and then *I* went into shock! But I knew God didn't want me in that situation.

I went back to my motel room and flopped on the bed. To tell you the truth, I was really discouraged. I had just turned down the solution to our unemployment problems. I had a chance to bring our personal recession to an end, but had passed on my opportunity. Now how in the world was I going to explain this to Mary?

That turned out to be the easy part. Mary's response over the phone from her hospital bed to all this was, "Steve, that's fine. We don't need to go there. God knows what He's doing, and He's the One who will take care of us." It helps to have a wife who has a grip on the sovereignty of God.

What didn't help was that the board called me back the next morning. They upped their salary offer, and get this: They offered to give us the money for a down payment on a house. Not loan us, but *give* us. Now I should point out that this was not a large church, but apparently several of the board members were doing rather well financially and had offered to personally participate in this more generous offer. I couldn't believe they were resorting to offering me more filthy lucre (to use the King James Version).

For a moment it didn't seem filthy at all. It was very tempting. And in no way were they trying to do something inappropriate. They were concerned that the financial package might not have been ample enough. But that really wasn't the case. They'd been more than generous in the original offer. The real issue for me wasn't finances, it was obedience.

I was still broke and without a job. Mary was still in the hospital in Atlanta, and things were still completely up in the air. (I'm writing this almost twenty years later, but I'm starting to get depressed all over again just from writing the story.)

DEPRESSION: DE-STRUCTURAL ENGINEERING

Let me pause in my story for a moment to take you back to a beautiful summer evening in Kansas City. It was a Friday night on July 17, 1981, and hundreds of people had gathered for a delightful evening of dancing to the big-band sounds of the forties. All sixteen hundred people were gathered in the atrium of the luxurious new Hyatt Regency.

But the great music, the beautiful fountains, and the festive atmosphere all came to a quick and grinding halt at 7:05 P.M. Suddenly, the dancers, musicians, waiters, and everyone else in the building stopped to pay attention to some sounds other than the music.

> Looking up toward the source of the sound, they saw two groups of people on the second- and fourth-floor walkways, observing the festivities and stomping in rhythm with the music. As the two walkways began to fall, the observers were seen holding on to the railings with terrified expressions on their faces. The fourth-floor walkway dropped from the hangers holding it to the roof structure, leaving the hangers dangling like impotent stalactites. Since the second-floor walkway hung from the fourth-floor walkway, the two began to fall together. There was a large roar as the concrete decks of the steel-framed walkways cracked and crashed down, in a billowing cloud of dust on the crowd gathered around the bar below the second-floor walkway. People were screaming; the west glass wall adjacent to the walkways shattered, sending shards of glass flying over 100 feet; pipes broken by the falling walkways sent jets of water spraying the atrium floor. It was a nightmare the survivors would never forget.
>
> The following day the press mentioned 44 dead and 82 injured.... The final count reported 114 dead and over 200 injured, many maimed for life. It was indeed the worst structural failure ever to occur in the United States."[1]

I think it would be fair to say that of those sixteen hundred who were gathered in the Hyatt Regency that beautiful Sunday evening, not one of them expected to be part of a disaster resulting from a structural defect. Can you imagine the emotions that the survivors of the tragedy had to work through? The ensuing grief, the terror, the nightmares, the fear of walking into other buildings. Now, so many years later, they're probably still dealing with the emotional fallout on a regular basis.

That's similar to what happens when someone falls into severe depression. The vast majority of people I know who have been through depression were absolutely shocked when their emotional walls and walkways began to crack and cave in. They were completely unprepared for the emotional disaster.

That's what depression is. It's an internal, emotional disaster that stems from too much stress on a given point in our emotional infrastructure. Those walkways in the Kansas City Hyatt Regency were designed to handle a certain amount of stress and weight. But obviously something went very wrong, and the structure wasn't able to handle the actual stress and strain that was put upon it. What happened that night when those walkways collapsed is a tragic but accurate illustration of what happens when depression comes into someone's life. The stress is greater than we were designed to handle, and the walls of our normal existence begin to cave in. That's why a depressed person can't "just get over it." It's a major, structural breakdown that takes time to repair. I know.

That's why I found myself sitting at that intersection in tears.

The emotional infrastructure was caving in after nearly a year of incredible stress, disappointment, and frustration. The most difficult aspect of all this for me was that I'd never been this way before. I'd never experienced anything remotely similar. I had no idea what was happening to me! I had no reference point by which to measure my emotional stress. As a result, I thought I was in much worse shape than I actually was. I thought I was on a fast track to a mental institution, but in actuality I was going through what most counselors would describe as "moderate" depression.

It may have been moderate to them, but it was severe to me.

That's sort of like surviving a "moderate earthquake." A moderate earthquake can be very severe. Especially if you're the only guy in town whose house falls down.

Everything has a stress limit. An eighteen-wheel semi going down the freeway has a much greater stress limit than a Honda Civic. That's why it's not unusual to see lines of trucks pulled off to the side of an interstate highway. At periodic spots on every interstate, trucks must stop at weigh stations. Every truck is weighed, and if the truck and its cargo are over the truck's specified stress limit, it's the end of the road.

Trucks have stress limits. Hanging walkways have stress limits. And people have stress limits. Perhaps you've seen the Homes-Rahe stress scale commonly employed by counselors. It has been determined that various changes that come into our lives have varying degrees of stress. Homes-Rahe assigns a point value to different events. For example, the death of a spouse is 100 points, a divorce is 73, a personal injury or illness is 53, a job dismissal is 47, change of career is 36, and a change in sleeping habits is 16.

What's funny is that going on a vacation will earn you 13 points, and just experiencing Christmas will get you 12! There are many more categories I don't have room to mention, each with its own point value.

Researchers have determined that an accumulation of 200 or more points in a single year will result in some type of physical or emotional breakdown. When I took the test, I didn't score 200; I scored 1200. I was 1000 points over the normal breaking point. No wonder I was crying at that intersection: I should have stopped at the weigh station.

Now I'm no professional counselor, but I dove into some books and began doing research on depression. I found out that, generally speaking, depression comes from some sort of loss in your life. The exception to this, of course, would be depression that stems from physical reasons, such as a chemical or hormonal imbalance. That wasn't my problem. My problem was that I'd undergone tremendous loss in that nine-month period of time. And each loss would bring its own special kind of stress. After a while, momentum began to build. Instead of shedding stress, I was picking up more with each passing week.

Eventually, my emotional walkway just collapsed.

Right there in that intersection.

Depression is especially tough on those of us who have always considered ourselves to be emotional eighteen-wheelers. (You know—sensitive as a Mack truck.) That's why depression is tough for so many guys. When I meet with a guy who looks like he's got it together, I have to remind myself that appearances can be very deceiving. In the privacy of a one-on-one conversation, I sometimes learn that this "got-it-together" guy is walking on the razor's edge of a breakdown.

That's a very tough place to be. Especially when you've never been there before. Up until now, you've always been able to carry the load, no matter how strenuous. But this time it's different. This time there's been a major collapse on the inside. And every morning you fight off the big, black dog (as Winston Churchill called his frequent battles with depression), Scotch-tape yourself together, and try to survive for another day.

The other thing that's so tough is that you begin to imagine you'll never get over it—that it will *always* be this way, that you'll *always* be under this pile. And when everyone else is doing fine and having a good time at a wedding, birthday, ball game, or some other event you used to completely enjoy, it's all you can do to fight off the overwhelming feelings of despair and hopelessness.

That's depression. And some of you reading this are right in the middle of it. In fact, you're up to your chin in it. The enemy will tell you that you won't pull out of it, that things will never change. I had lunch several weeks ago with a businessman who was starting to believe that. No one would have guessed as we walked into the coffee shop that this guy was anything but a big-time success. Tall, good-looking, athletic build, early forties, he certainly looked as though he had life wired. We sat down at a table over in the corner, away from everyone else. And that's where he told me that just the night before, he'd come within a quarter-inch squeeze of his trigger finger from taking his own life.

His teenage daughter was running with the wrong crowd, he had suffered a major financial reversal, and he was just about to lose his home. Not to mention the strain that all these things were putting on his marriage. He'd become convinced that things would never change, would never get better. It was only the grace of God that kept him from sending a bullet through his brain that night.

The bottom line of his despair? He felt sure God had abandoned him.

I remember those feelings of abandonment. I remember those two years when the only part of Scripture I could read was the Psalms. I would often turn to a certain spot in Psalm 77. (I realize that we looked at this in a previous chapter, but I want to do it this time with a little different twist.) When I was going through my rough time, there were particular phrases that would get my full and undivided attention, for those were the verses I related to when things were so bleak and dark. I've highlighted those verses in bold print. It goes like this.

My voice rises to God, and I will cry aloud;
My voice rises to God, and He will hear me.

In the day of my trouble I sought the Lord;
In the night my hand was stretched out without weariness;
My soul refused to be comforted.
When I remember God, then I am disturbed;

When I sigh, then my spirit grows faint. Selah.

You have held my eyelids open;
I am so troubled that I cannot speak.

I have considered the days of old,
The years of long ago.
I will remember my song in the night;
I will meditate with my heart,
And my spirit ponders:

Will the Lord reject forever?
And will He never be favorable again?
Has His lovingkindness ceased forever?
Has His promise come to an end forever?
Has God forgotten to be gracious,
Or has He in anger withdrawn His compassion? Selah.

Then I said "It is my grief,
That the right hand of the Most High has changed." (Psalm 77:1–10)

I think this psalm poignantly captures the conflicting emotions of some-one struggling with depression. What makes it even more interesting is that it's a godly man struggling with depression. And it's recorded in the Bible.

There are a lot of us who love Jesus Christ who can relate to Psalm 77. I think that most Christians, at some point in their lives, will find themselves in depressing situations that drive them to the Psalms. And there are some nights that are so tough that only Psalm 77 offers any relief. At least part of that relief is the realization that somebody on this planet has been as bad off as I am.

Let's quickly summarize what this guy is saying:

- His soul *refuses* to be comforted. It doesn't get any tougher than that.
- When he remembers God, he doesn't get relief; he gets even more stressed out!
- He's so overloaded with difficulty that he can't get any sleep. And he blames it on God! (*You* have held my eyelids open).
- He is so locked up inside with frustration, disappointment, and grief that he can't even speak. Or pray. (Have you ever been there?)

Then he begins to think some wild thoughts. Thoughts like:

- God has rejected me, and it looks like this rejection is permanent.
- God has put me permanently on the shelf. (He'll *never* be favorable again.)
- God's lovingkindness has ceased to exist in my life. And all the evi-dence seems to indicate that this is going to be a *long*-term condition.
- I used to count on God's promises, but all I've got in my life now are broken promises.
- God has completely abandoned me. He has forgotten about me. He has not been gracious to me; He is against me.

- All of this is my fault. God is punishing me for something I've done. He's angry with me. That's why all of this stuff is happening to me.
- And He's not letting up one bit. He obviously has no compassion toward me or my situation. If He did, I wouldn't be feeling so rotten.

I've heard it said that Christians shouldn't ever get depressed. I didn't read that in the Bible. I didn't read it in the Old Testament or in the New Testament. You can't find it in Paul's writings. But I do remember hearing it from someone. Someone who had never personally dealt with depression.

Come to think of it, it was me.

I was the one who said it. I said it *before* I went through my depression. But then I found myself right in the middle of an unscheduled pit stop. A pit stop that had me drowning in a depression. And I had no idea that the worst was yet to come. I had thought the blast furnace was hot already, but it was only getting cranked up.

As Paul Harvey would say, that's the rest of the story.

EIGHT

TOTALED OUT

PART 2

When you come to the bottom, you find God.

NEVILLE TALBOT

IF YOU RECALL FROM OUR LAST EPISODE…I'd been floundering in the fires of depression and impossible circumstances until the steel in my soul seemed the consistency of tomato soup. Mary was still in the hospital in Atlanta. As I headed for Atlanta on the plane, those feelings of depression started to roll over me again, like fog billowing through the Golden Gate Bridge.

Now what? I asked myself. *I've got a wife in the hospital, two kids living with their grandparents, no job, and no place to go.*

Well, that wasn't quite right. I did have one other place to go.

But to be honest, I didn't want to go there.

I mentioned earlier that, in my four years of pastoring, I had never received one call of inquiry from another church until after I resigned. That's not quite true. I did receive a call from one church. They were looking for a senior pastor. I remember thinking to myself after hanging up the receiver, "I would *never* go to that church." Some people think God doesn't have a sense of humor. That certainly hasn't been my experience.

After I had resigned, this same church called me again. And once again, I told them I wasn't interested; I was talking to "other" churches. Even so, they continued to call, and I continued to say no. The way I saw it, it wasn't even close to being a match. I was a young buck in my early thirties; they were a church with an average age closer to seventy. They were on a small, landlocked piece of property with no room for expansion, and any nearby acreage was priced out of reality.

I had an immediate interest in all the other churches that had contacted me. But not with this one. I'll give you one guess where I wound up. I didn't see a future there.

But God did.

When I got to Atlanta, Mary and I discussed this little church that I'd turned down so many times. Maybe, just maybe, this was a place we should consider after all. Maybe God had closed the door on all those other options because He wanted us to take a serious look at an option we didn't even think was in the ball game. Mary and I talked and prayed, and talked and prayed some more. What made it even more difficult was that I'd filled the pulpit for this church on several Sundays while they were continuing their search. And the last time I preached for them, I had publicly thanked them for their invitation, but told them I was sure God was leading me in another direction.

"Mary, they're going to think I'm nuts if I call them back and tell them I'm open to coming."

"Steve," she replied, "if God is in this, He'll take care of their response."

And that's just what He did. I dialed their number, and the response was truly amazing. The church officer told me they'd decided on Wednesday night not to take my no as final. They had spent the entire Wednesday in prayer, asking God to change my mind. They were praying as I was meeting with the elders from the other church to tell them yes. We now knew where we were going and the crisis was over, right? I wish that were the case, but we were just getting warmed up. I went back to California to find us a place to live and to get things squared away for Mary. Mary needed to stay in Atlanta for another month before she was able to travel. Before I left Atlanta, we had a long talk with the doctor about Mary's condition.

Generally speaking, he was optimistic. But he did mention that it would be unwise for Mary to get pregnant any time in the coming year. She was on medication to break down the clot which had lodged in the abdominal region, and a pregnancy would only complicate the healing process. Especially with the clot in that area of her body. He told us that if she got pregnant during that time, she could wind up in the hospital for most of the pregnancy.

Well, three months later the second immaculate conception took place. Excuse my levity, but we could not believe it. We had been very, very careful. Careful to the point of irritation in my opinion! And Mary winds up pregnant. Unbelievable! But the way things had been going, it seemed to be par for the course.

Shortly after we learned of Mary's pregnancy, I was in my new office getting things organized. Unaccountably, I felt a sharp headache coming on right after lunch. I usually don't get headaches, so I took a couple of Tylenol and figured that would take care of it. An hour went by and nothing changed, so I took two more Tylenol. Nothing. So I decided to go home early and try to grab a short nap because we were going to a banquet that evening. I took some more Tylenol when I got home. Nothing. We went to the banquet and things got worse. I developed a fever while I was eating dinner. As soon as it was appropriate, I excused myself and went home. I took two more Tylenol before I hit the sheets.

At two o'clock that morning I woke up with a temperature of 103 and an absolutely unbelievable headache. This was more than some flu bug. I decided I'd better go in and see a doctor.

When I got to the emergency room, I had to wait. What's new, right? When they finally put me in that little white-walled room I had to wait some more. By the time the doctor walked in, it was nearly four in the morning.

Have you ever seen an emergency room doctor at four in the morning? This guy looked terrible—like he hadn't slept in three weeks. He was a mess...and *he* was going to try and help me? I felt so sorry for him, I told him he'd better lie down for a while.

Right off the top, he started peppering me with all kinds of questions. Then he put me through a series of exercises. I found myself getting just a little irritated; I wasn't there for aerobics, just some antibiotics.

Then he got my undivided attention when he said, "I think you've got meningitis."

Meningitis?

I couldn't believe my ears.

Let me tell you how I felt at that moment. I felt like a quarterback who took the snap, dropped back to pass, and then had *my own* linemen come after me to sack me. I couldn't believe God would let this happen. With everything we'd been through that year; including unemployment; Mary's two surgeries; a staggering hospital bill; Mary at home in bed, pregnant and recovering from phlebitis; and I've got meningitis!

I didn't have time for meningitis.

I didn't have the money for meningitis.

I didn't have the emotional energy it takes to go through meningitis.

The doctor then told me there were two strains of the virus. He thought I had the least severe type, but he wasn't sure. He told me they would do a procedure and know in twenty minutes what the diagnosis actually was. The procedure was a spinal tap. I wasn't real excited about that, especially since it is a delicate procedure and this guy didn't look real sharp. Twenty minutes later he came back in.

"The results were inconclusive," he said.

"What does that mean?" I asked.

"We took a culture and we won't know the results for seventy-two hours."

"You mean I have to wait here for *three days* to find out what kind of meningitis I have?"

"That's correct."

"What if it does turn out that I have the worst kind of meningitis?"

"Well, if that's the case, we'd have to have your wife and kids in to go through the same procedure that you did."

I couldn't believe it. So for three days I was in the hospital. And for three days I got to play the "what if" game. I lay there in my bed and thought through all the worst-case scenarios. After what I'd been through that year, it seemed like a logical exercise. You play the "what if" game as you think through all of the worst options that could come out of your current circumstances. "What if" this happens, or "what if" that happens? It's a very slow kind of mental torture. But in those circumstances, it's also pretty normal.

I finally got some good news on Monday morning. The doctor came in and told me that everything was under control. I could go home. I can't tell you what a relief that was. The waiting was over! We were off the hook and the antibiotics would do the job!

I was in a great mood for about three hours. Until Mary walked in.

The moment she walked in the door, I knew something was wrong. Big-time wrong. Her face was about as white as the sheet on my hospital bed. She had just come from seeing a specialist at Stanford. Since her pregnancy involved an existing clot, she was seeing a vascular surgeon who specialized in obstetrics.

Mary proceeded to tell me about the visit. The doctor was very concerned about the medication Mary had been taking to break down the clot. Of course, she was taking it before she knew she was pregnant. And that was the concern.

He told her there was a very good chance that the medication had affected our unborn child in the early days of pregnancy. The baby could very well be deformed. He suggested that Mary have an abortion. Mary made it very clear to him that abortion was not an option for us. He replied by pointing out that we already had a healthy girl and a healthy boy, so why take an unnecessary chance?

Quite frankly, this doctor was pressing Mary very hard. She came back just as firmly. Finally, in frustration with her responses, he said to her, "All I can tell you is that you're probably going to have a little monster." (This guy had a great bedside manner.)

Just that quickly, we were back on the ash heap again. At least I'd had two or three hours of relief. Now we were facing something much bigger than anything else we had faced to that point. And we had to wait, not seventy-two hours, but *seven months* to see what the outcome would be.

Let me jump ahead and finish the story. Mary never spent a single day in the hospital, except to have Josh. And when he was born, he was perfect. Now, it could have turned out that he was born handicapped. That would have been very difficult, but it would have been okay. We're all born handicapped to one degree or another. Nevertheless, God, the giver of life, chose to bless us with a healthy little boy. Now, maybe he would grow up to be a monster (that's a joke for Josh). But that didn't happen. Josh is now eighteen and a young man we're very proud of.

DIFFICULT LESSONS

Although it took me two years to fully emerge from my depression, God taught me some invaluable lessons during that period of time. It was within the pages of that three-year chapter that I really learned how to begin the process of trusting God. There were some character flaws in my life that God wanted to adjust. And there are some things that are only changed through tremendous pressure.

That hard chapter did come to an end. But now, as we look back on it eighteen years later, we see it as one of the most worthwhile and necessary chapters we've ever endured. Yes, it was difficult. Bitterly difficult. But God was accomplishing something extremely valuable in our lives and in our marriage.

When Mary and I were going through this tough passage of our lives, we made it a practice to request two things from the Lord. First, we asked Him to teach us everything that He had for us in this experience. I can't speak for Mary, but I prayed that prayer because I didn't want to have to go through something like this again. I wanted to get it the first time around!

Second, we prayed that God would take our difficulty and somehow use it to minister to others. God has answered that prayer above and beyond anything we could ever ask or think. This book is a case in point. I never would have dreamed back then that I would one day share this story in a book to other people who are hurting. I was so far down in those days that the thought of publishing a book would have seemed like a crazy dream. And the thought that this would be my ninth book would have been completely laughable. You see, when you're in the pit, you think you're finished. I hoped that one day I might be able to minister to a few people out of our pit. But thousands of people have heard this story in person, and thousands more will read it in these pages.

To those of you who are reading this and finding yourselves in the toughest chapter of your life, let me encourage you to ask God for the same things that Mary and I asked Him for. Ask Him to show you everything He wants you to learn in this difficult experience. And then ask Him to some-how use it in the life of someone else.

Looking back across my life, I can see that I made a big mistake when I was ten years old. When I was ten, I knelt at an altar on a Sunday night in our church and asked God to use me. I had no idea what I was asking for, and if I had, I probably wouldn't have asked.

One of my all-time favorite books is called *The Tapestry*, written by Edith Schaeffer. It's the story of Francis and Edith Schaeffer and the remarkable work God did through them and their ministry in Switzerland.

As I was perusing the book, I noticed a section that was underlined from my first reading ten years prior. Edith Schaeffer penned these profound words:

> Never forget this…at any point in life, in a thousand different kinds of situations, the *answer* to the prayer, "Use me, Lord, I want to be greatly used of Thee," can be the hardest thing you have ever faced. It is the answer to prayer that brings exhaustion of a variety of kinds, and that brings a cost to be paid that almost smashes you, and me. There is always a cost to being "used mightily for the Lord…."[1]

Those words impacted me, for I immediately realized that I had read them for the first time just a few weeks before my "crushing experience" commenced. They held much greater meaning for me this time than they did the first time I read them. Now I could see how God had answered that prayer of a ten-year-old boy—but answered it in a way I would have never imagined.

I have two advanced theological degrees. That's really no big deal. It just means you're able to read a few books and pass some tests. I went after those degrees for one reason: I believed they would equip me for ministry. But do you know what I discovered?

Theological degrees don't equip you for ministry.

What equips you for ministry is suffering.

Have you ever asked God to use you? Have you ever asked God to make your life count? Have you ever asked God to work through you and speak through you in a significant way in the life of someone else? I hope you realize that "ministry" is not restricted to those who are in "full-time" ministry. All of us are ambassadors of Christ.

Stop and think about it. Have you asked God to really pick you up and use you as a tool for His kingdom purposes? Then that should help explain why you find yourself in the midst of a crushing experience. God is equipping you to minister to someone else at a future time. That's the clear message of 2 Corinthians 1:3–4:

> Praise be to the God and Father of our Lord Jesus Christ, the Father of compassion and the God of all comfort, who comforts us in all our troubles, so that we can comfort those in any trouble with the comfort we ourselves have received from God. (NIV)

IDENTIFICATION

Years ago, a man stood with a telephone receiver in his hand, unwilling to believe what the voice on the other end was telling him. His nineteen-year-old son, while riding his motorcycle, had collided head-on with a car. The doctor told him to get to the hospital as quickly as possible, since his son's condition was critical.

As the man raced into the hospital room, he suddenly stopped in shock and disbelief. One look told him that his son was dead. The doctor walked over to him and quietly whispered, "I'm sorry," and then left him to be alone with his departed son.

Shock, grief, denial. All of those emotions played havoc in his heart as he cradled the lifeless hand of his son. Minutes later, he heard the door crack open. He turned to see the pastor of his church. The *new* pastor of his church. The pastor was literally moving into his office when he got the call from the hospital.

When the man saw the pastor, all of the anger came boiling to the surface. "Where was God when my boy was killed?" he raged at the pastor. The pastor stepped back, and then he was silent for several long moments. Very gently he replied, "I think He was in the same place that He was when my boy was killed."

Suddenly where there had been a wall, there was now a bridge. It is suffering that equips us for ministry.

If you are crushed, if you are depressed, if you are broken, you should know this: All God is doing is answering your prayer. He is getting ready to use you significantly. And as you experience His healing and comfort in your own life, there will come a day when He will bring someone across your path—someone in the deep, dark depths of a pit. And as he tells you about that trapdoor that opened beneath his feet, as he pours out his anguish and pain, he may at some point say, "I know this must be difficult for you to understand."

Then you can tell him your story…and then he will know that it isn't difficult at all for you to understand. For you have been where he is now. And God will use you in a way that you could never have been used without your season of suffering. In that very moment, you will experience firsthand the fruit of your hardship.

TWO POINTS OF PERSPECTIVE

It is a hard, hard thing to be crushed.

Psalm 34:18 tells us, "The LORD is near to the brokenhearted and saves those who are crushed in spirit."

Have you been crushed in your spirit? It may be from your circumstances, which seem so hopelessly twisted and distorted. It may be from a friend, a close friend, who has betrayed your trust or your confidence. It may be from an abusive parent or spouse. It may be from an unceasing battle with cancer. Whatever the circumstances, the fact of the matter is this. You've been crushed like an egg in the jaws of a vise, and you are so very, very tired of the broken heart which never stops aching.

My friend, the Lord has not forgotten you. You may feel that way, but He hasn't. He is near to you, nearer than you can imagine. And He will save you. If He could save you from sin, He can save you from hurt.

He may not do it on your time schedule, but He will do it. He is not only close to you, but He knows exactly what He is doing in your life. He's only getting you ready for something that you cannot see. He has a plan for you that would absolutely stagger you if you could see it. But you can't see it.

And that's probably for the best. For if you could see what He has in store for you, you couldn't handle it anyway. It would literally be too much for you.

These days I have two verses tacked on my bulletin board, just behind my computer. They remind me of what is true when I start to lose perspective. The first one is Isaiah 64:4.

"No eye has seen a God like you,
who works for those who wait for him!" (NLT)

The second is Jeremiah 31:3.

"I have loved you with an everlasting love;
therefore I have continued my faithfulness to you." (RSV)

Sometimes we're so caught up with the conflict within us and around us that we don't even realize that God is being faithful. The reason we don't realize it is because His faithfulness isn't readily apparent. But that doesn't mean it isn't there.

Elmer Bendiner flew numerous bombing runs over Germany in World War II. In his book *The Fall of Fortresses* he recalls one bombing run that he will never forget.

Our B-17 (*The Tondelayo*) was barraged by flak from Nazi antiaircraft guns. That was not unusual, but on this particular occasion our gas tanks were hit. Later, as I reflected on the miracle of a twenty-millimeter shell piercing the fuel tank without touching off an explosion, our pilot, Bohn Fawkes, told me it was not quite that simple.

On the morning following the raid, Bohn had gone down to ask our crew chief for that shell as a souvenir of unbelievable luck. The crew chief told Bohn that not just one shell but eleven had been found in the gas tanks—eleven unexploded shells where only one was sufficient to blast us out of the sky. It was as if the sea had parted for us. Even after thirty-five years, so awesome an event leaves me shaken, especially after I heard the rest of the story from Bohn.

He was told that the shells had been sent to the armorers to be defused. The armorers told him that Intelligence had picked them up. They could not say why at the time, but Bohn eventually sought out the answer.

Apparently, when the armorers opened each of those shells, they found no explosive charge. They were clean as a whistle and just as harmless. Empty? Not all of them.

One contained a carefully rolled piece of paper. On it was a scrawl in Czech. The Intelligence people scoured our base for a man who could reach Czech. Eventually, they found one to decipher the note. It set us marveling. Translated, the note read: "This is all we can do for you now."[2]

If you are in the pit as you read these words, I wish that I could somehow throw you a rope and pull you out of there. If you are crushed from the weight of overcoming circumstances, I wish there was a way I could roll that weight off your shoulders. But I can't.

All I can do is point you to the One who was faithful to us when we were in the deepest pit of our lives. He was faithful to us. He will be faithful to you.

That is all I can say to you for now.

NINE

GETTING THE BIG HEAD

I hope I shall possess firmness and virtue enough
to maintain what I consider the most enviable of all titles,
the character of an honest man.

GEORGE WASHINGTON

IF ISRAEL HAD A MOUNT RUSHMORE, you can bet that David's head would be one of the four faces carved into the mountainside.

It would be interesting to speculate who else might be up there. Abraham? Moses? Elijah? If I had a shot at it, I think I might cast a vote for King Josiah.

But there's no doubt at all: David was one of the greatest of the great. Even so, I have a strong feeling that David wouldn't care much at all about that sort of honor. There was another honor that meant a lot more to the son of Jesse. And there was another hill that captured his heart more than Mount Rushmore ever could.

It's the hill described in Psalm 15—the hill of integrity.

We'll be taking the measure of that towering slope on the biblical landscape in this chapter. One of the reasons that God has for taking a man through the pit is to develop his integrity. A man who stands tall on the hill of integrity has usually gotten there by going through some kind of pit.

A BIG HEAD FOR TED

You've heard of someone getting a big head.

That's what Mount Rushmore is all about.

Mount Rushmore has the distinction of bestowing the big head on four former presidents of the United States. You've seen pictures, I'm sure, of the magnificent sculpture that Gutzon Borglum and his crew blasted and carved out of the granite cliff in the Black Hills of South Dakota. But pictures don't do justice to that great stone monument. I had a chance to visit there last spring. And the grandeur of that massive sculpture takes your breath away.

George Washington, Thomas Jefferson, Abraham Lincoln, and Theodore Roosevelt all got the big heads. And I do mean big. Each head is the size of a five-story building (that's approximately *sixty* feet high).

Washington, Lincoln, and Roosevelt would have gotten my vote for the big head, but personally, I would have opted for John Adams over Thomas Jefferson. When I think of Jefferson, I can't help recalling that he had the gall to publish his own bible. He edited out the parts of the real Bible that he didn't agree with—including the teachings of the Lord Jesus—and then published his "superior version." There were, and still are, some serious questions about Jefferson's character. But the character of Washington, Lincoln, and Teddy Roosevelt is, to this day, above reproach.

Of those three presidents, Theodore Roosevelt was the most recent to serve (1901–1909), but to our generation he is relatively unknown. George Grant introduces us to one of the greatest of all American presidents:

> By any measure Theodore Roosevelt was a remarkable man. Before his fiftieth birthday he had served as a New York state legislator, the under-secretary of the Navy, police commissioner for the city of New York, U.S. civil service commissioner, the governor of the state of New York, the vice-president under William McKinley, a colonel in the U.S. Army, and two terms as the president of the United States.[1]

That's an amazing résumé for someone only fifty years old. I'm fifty-one and I got tired just reading that paragraph. Grant continues:

> In addition, he had run a cattle ranch in the Dakota Territories, served as a reporter and editor for several scientific journals, news-

papers, and magazines, and conducted scientific expeditions on four continents. He read at least five books every week of his life and wrote nearly fifty on an astonishing array of subjects—from history and biography to natural science and social criticism.

He enjoyed hunting, boxing and wrestling. He was an amateur taxidermist, botanist, ornithologist, and astronomer. He was a devoted family man who lovingly raised six children. And he enjoyed a lifelong romance with his wife."[2]

Are you starting to pick up the flavor of this man's life? Here was a leader, a man of action, and a man in love with life. He loved his Lord and he loved his family. Teddy Roosevelt said, "The greatest privilege, the greatest duty for any man is to be happily married."[3]

Theodore Roosevelt had many friends and adversaries. Here's a sampling of what they had to say about the youngest man ever to become president in the United States of America.

During his long and varied career, he was hailed by supporters and rivals alike as the greatest man of the age—perhaps of all the ages …President Grover Cleveland described him as "one of the ablest men yet produced in human history." Senator Henry Cabot Lodge asserted that, "Since Caesar, perhaps no one has attained among crowded duties and great responsibilities, such high proficiency in so many separate fields of activity." After an evening in his company, the epic poet Rudyard Kipling wrote, "I curled up on the seat opposite and listened and wondered until the universe seemed to be spinning round—and Roosevelt was the spinner." Great Britain's Lord Charnwood exclaimed, "No statesman for centuries has had his width of intellectual range; to be sure no intellectual has so touched the world with action."

Even Roosevelt's lifelong political opponent, William Jennings Bryan, was bedazzled by his prowess. "Search the annals of history if you will," he said. "Never will you find a man more remarkable in every way than he."[4]

It's one thing for your friends to say glowing things about you. It's quite another for a political foe to pay you that kind of compliment. Theodore Roosevelt was the real thing. Throughout his life, however, he remained quite unimpressed with himself. In writing about his talents, he described himself simply as "an ordinary man":

In most things I am just about average; in some of them a little under, rather than over. I am only an ordinary walker. I can't run. I am not a good swimmer, although I am a strong one. I probably ride better than anything else I do, but I am certainly not a remarkably good rider. I am not a good shot. I never could be a good boxer, although I do keep at it, whenever I can. My eyesight prevents me from ever being a good tennis player, even if otherwise I could qualify. I am not a brilliant writer. I have written a great deal, but I always have to work and slave over everything I write. The things I have done are all, with the possible exception of the Panama Canal, just such things as any ordinary man could have done. There is nothing brilliant or outstanding in my record at all."[5]

That is a refreshing self-analysis by a very gifted man. There is something in that description that is utterly foreign—and nearly extinct—among too many politicians.

I refer to a virtue known as *humility*.

Another great aspect of Theodore Roosevelt was his courage. Early in his political career, he took on the corrupt political bosses of New York. Warned of the dangers of such a confrontation, he never hesitated to bring down corruption wherever he found it.

He led his men into a hail of Spanish bullets as they charged up San Juan Hill. While on safari in Africa, Teddy stood his ground against a male rhinoceros in full charge. TR calmly lifted his rifle, took aim, and squeezed off a shot. The bullet took the rhino through the brain at fifty yards. On another excursion, he shot a mountain lion *while hanging upside down* over a cliff— with a worried Secret Service agent holding his feet.

But it was his political courage that so astonished the people of his day.

Whenever he had something unpleasant to say, he always seemed to find a way to say it to the most unsympathetic audience—he stated his commitment to the gold standard in the heart of the pro-silver belt; he defended the rigid New York blue laws in a downtown saloon district; he publicly rebuked the governor of Arkansas, sitting on the platform next to him, because he had implicationally defended racist lynchings; he condemned the rebels against British rule in an address in Cairo, though he had been warned that he would be shot if he even brought up the issue; and he received his friend Booker T. Washington on a dais in Jackson, Mississippi.[6]

Where did all of this courage and character come from in the life of Theodore Roosevelt? We might find one significant clue in one of the great man's favorite passages in the Bible, Micah 6:8:

He has told you, O man, what is good;
And what does the LORD require of you
But to do justice, to love kindness,
And to walk humbly with your God?

In 1917, the New York Bible Society asked Roosevelt to pen a word of encouragement to the young soldiers heading off to fight in World War I. Each soldier was to be given a pocket New Testament with the former president's words included in each small Bible as a preface. What Roosevelt wrote became known as "The Micah Mandate."

He told the soldiers that the entire New Testament was actually fore-shadowed in Micah 6:8.[7] He challenged the young men to live their lives and to do their soldiering according to principles of God's Word:

Do justice, and therefore fight valiantly against those that stand for the reign of Moloch and Beelzebub on this earth. Love mercy; treat your enemies well, succor the afflicted; treat every woman as if she were your sister; care for the little children; and be tender with the old and helpless. Walk humbly; and you will do so if you study the life and teachings of the Savior, walking in his steps.[8]

"Treat every woman as if she were your sister."

That's a refreshing word of advice to come from a president who presided in the Oval Office with honor. Young female interns in Washington D.C. have nothing to fear from elected officials who follow Roosevelt's advice and example.

As a former commander in chief, Roosevelt was encouraging those young soldiers not only to follow his words, but also his personal example. His talk was congruent with his walk. It all added up in the life of Theodore Roosevelt because he was a man of principle. He actually believed in something.

He would have been astonished at the idea of taking a poll to find out what people wanted to hear. He didn't *care* what they wanted to hear. And the reason he didn't care is because he didn't worry about staying in office. On one occasion he stated, "My success so far has only been won by absolute indifference to my future career."[9] He had no interest in winning a future election if it meant that he must sacrifice truth and doing the right thing.

"I do not believe," Theodore Roosevelt stated, "that any man should ever attempt to make politics his only career. It is a dreadful misfortune for a man to grow to feel that his whole livelihood and whole happiness depend upon his staying in office. Such a feeling prevents him from being of real service to the people while in office and always puts him under the heaviest strain of pressure to barter his convictions for the sake of holding office."[10]

That paragraph drips with unimpeachable integrity. If you have that kind of character, you don't need to ever worry about being impeached. *Unimpeachable* means completely trustworthy, not open to doubt or question. But if you lack that kind of integrity, well, that's impeachable. And we've had enough of that.

Teddy Roosevelt had unimpeachable integrity.

George Washington had the same thing.

And Abraham Lincoln was known as Honest Abe. Not corrupt Abe, not lying Abe, not sexual predator Abe. *Honest* Abe.

That's why they got the big heads. Not big heads of ego, but big heads of honor. They were honored on Mount Rushmore for their character and integrity. Thomas Jefferson doesn't quite make the cut of character and integrity. But three out of four isn't bad.

That's how they made it to the hill known as Mount Rushmore.

THE BIG HILL

The last I heard, they're no longer taking applications for another big head on Mount Rushmore. That particular national monument is closed to any more five-story granite profiles. But there is another hill—that all-important hill I mentioned a few pages ago. The hill of which I speak is the Big Hill. And David, the psalmist, had some eloquent things to say about it as he climbed its slopes:

> O LORD, who may abide in Your tent?
> Who may dwell on Your holy hill?
> He who walks with integrity, and works righteousness,
> And speaks truth in his heart.
> He does not slander with his tongue,
> Nor does evil to his neighbor,
> Nor takes up a reproach against his friend;
> In whose eyes a reprobate is despised,
> But who honors those who fear the LORD;
> He swears to his own hurt and does not change;
> He does not put out his money at interest,
> Nor does he take a bribe against the innocent.
> He who does these things will never be shaken. (Psalm 15)

This is a tougher hill to ascend than Mount Rushmore. When you read down through this integrity sketch, it's really a description of the Lord Jesus Christ. He's the only One who perfectly fits this list. Nevertheless, by God's grace, we are being conformed to the very image of Christ (Romans 8:29). And the more Christlike I become, the more that change is going to be evident in my behavior and in my integrity.

Did you notice that this psalm opens with a question?

O LORD, who may abide in Your tent?
Who may dwell on Your holy hill? (v. 1)

There are two key word couplings in that verse: *abide-tent* and *dwell-hill*.

Now what is this all about? Well, let me ask you a question. Who abides in your tent? You say you don't have a tent? Then who dwells in your condominium, or your apartment, or your house? The answer is family members. Family members abide in your home. Sometimes you have guests, but they only stay for a few days. But your family abides in your tent, or house, or condo.

Here's another question. Who dwells on your hill? You say that you don't have a hill? Well, then who lives on your property? Once again, the answer is family.

So in essence, the question being asked is, "Lord, who may be in Your family and abide in Your tent and live on Your property?" The answer takes up the rest of the psalm; each of the remaining four verses answers that question. Verse 2 gets right to heart of the matter: *"He who walks with integrity."*

Integrity is at the very heart of the issue. That's what God is looking for. Now all of us have a major problem here and the problem is something called *sin*. Sin is missing the mark, falling short of God's standard. And, according to the Bible, all of us had done that.

Romans 3:23 states, "For all have sinned and fall short of the glory of God." So right out of the blocks, we're in big trouble. The chances of us dwelling on God's holy hill, on God's Mount Rushmore, are slim and none. And Slim just slipped out the back door.

We have a major dilemma on our hands. That's why Romans 6:23 is such great, backslapping news: "For the wages of sin is death, but the free gift of God is eternal life in Jesus Christ our Lord."

So how do we obtain this free gift that takes away our sin and give us eternal life?

If you confess with your mouth Jesus as Lord, and believe in your heart that God raised Him from the dead, you shall be saved; for with the heart a person believes, resulting in righteousness, and with the mouth he confesses, resulting in salvation. For the Scripture says, "WHOEVER BELIEVES IN HIM WILL NOT BE DISAPPOINTED." (Romans 10:9–11)

When we follow those Scriptures from our hearts, ask Christ to come into our lives, and give control of our lives over to Him, the sin problem is taken away. It is removed by the fact that I am now justified by the blood of Christ. My sin is paid for by Christ in full. Past, present, and future.

But now that I'm a new creation, I am called to walk along a new trail. I am to follow Christ on the trail of righteousness. Having experienced spiritual birth, I must now begin to learn spiritual *growth*. God doesn't want me to remain an infant forever. He wants me to grow and develop spiritually, just as a pediatrician gives a child a physical each year to make sure he's growing physically.

The Lord wants me to grow in grace. He wants me to be conformed to the image of Christ. He wants the Word of God to be lived out in my private life and in my public life. And that takes us back to verse 2 and the whole issue of integrity. So who is it again who can abide in God's tent and dwell on His holy hill? The answer is clearly outlined in the rest of the psalm, beginning with verse 3. God expects His men to be growing and maturing in their integrity.

David didn't have this integrity thing down 100 percent—not by a long shot. And neither do we. But it must be something that remains very, very important to us—something we're constantly watching over in our lives. We need much grace to be men of integrity. Integrity is a valuable and precious commodity, and must be protected at all costs. You don't ever want to give up your integrity. You just can't afford to do it.

A LIFE THAT MATCHES YOUR WORDS

Let's take another pass at verse 2 of Psalm 15, as it provides the answer to the question of verse 1:

O LORD, who may abide in Your tent?
Who may dwell on Your holy hill?
He who walks with integrity, and works righteousness,
And speaks truth in his heart.

If you speak truth in your heart, it should be worked out in your life. When the representatives of the original thirteen colonies got together in Philadelphia to discuss uniting and breaking away from England, the issue of slavery was a difficult one. Obviously, the Southern states based their very economy on slavery. But even though the northern colonies spoke against slavery, it was widespread among them as well.

John Hancock, the president of the Continental Congress, "had only in recent years freed the last of the slaves who were part of his lavish Boston household."[11] "Even Benjamin Franklin, who adamantly opposed slavery, had once owned two black house servants and had personally traded slaves, buying and selling from his Market Street print shop."[12]

Benjamin Rush, a young and upcoming Philadelphia physician, was not a delegate to the Continental Congress, but would soon be elected to Congress from Philadelphia. In 1773, Rush had first come to public prominence when he published a very popular booklet that attacked slavery in the strongest of terms. The next year, he became one of the founders of the Pennsylvania Society for Promoting the Abolition of Slavery. He urged preachers to speak against its evils from their pulpits, and taught that blacks should have the same rights as whites, as both were created in the image of God. Even so, it was common knowledge in Philadelphia that Benjamin Rush owned his own personal slave.[13] It's an understatement to say that something was out of kilter.

Where is the integrity in speaking against slavery and owning a slave? The pieces just don't add up. Contrast Benjamin Rush's example with that of Robert E. Lee. As you know, Lee headed up the Confederate forces in the Civil War. That means Lee was for slavery, right? Not necessarily:

While fighting on the side of the slave-holding states seceding from
the Union, Lee fought neither for the right to own slaves nor even

for the right to secession. Indeed, he regarded the latter as "nothing less than revolution"—and Lee was not a revolutionary. As for slavery, Lee had his entire life believed in gradual emancipation. In his own affairs, he had no slaves of his own and freed every slave he inherited from his father-in-law before the Union attempted to enforce the Emancipation Proclamation on the seceded Southern states. More than that, he made every effort to ensure that the slaves under his care were freed under circumstances where they could support themselves—a step he believed that abolitionists driven by zealotry failed to consider.[14]

Lee was as clear in his denouncement of slavery as Benjamin Rush: "In this enlightened age, there are few I believe, but what will acknowledge that slavery as an institution, is a moral and political evil in any country. It is useless to expatiate on its disadvantages. I think it however a greater evil to the white than to the black race."[15]

Rush spoke out against slavery and had a slave. Lee spoke out against slavery, freed his inherited slaves, and gave them vocational training so they could support themselves and their families.

So who had the integrity?

TONGUE-LASHING

C. H. Spurgeon said that "some men's tongues bite more than their teeth." That's what verse 3, in essence, is all about:

He does not slander with his tongue,
Nor does evil to his neighbor,
Nor takes up a reproach against his friend.

Spurgeon is priceless on this verse. "The tongue is not steel," the great preacher writes, "but it cuts, and its wounds are very hard to heal; the worst wounds are not with its edge to our face, but to our back when our head is turned."[16]

My first inclination when I read that was to think about others who have done that to me. But then I remembered that not forty-eight hours ago, I spoke evil of a friend behind his back. I said it to my wife, who pointed out fairly quickly what I was doing. Then I got angry with *her* for loving me enough to tell me the truth. I had to clear all that up first thing this morning. But it took me two days to come around.

That's not good. Not good at all.

It's so easy to fall into this trap. It can even happen to men who got the big head.

In the center of Richmond's Capital Square stands a monument to three of Virginia's greatest sons, and three of America's greatest heroes: George Washington, Thomas Jefferson, and Patrick Henry. George Washington is seated upon his steed and flanked by the standing figures of Thomas Jefferson and Patrick Henry. Each member of this talented trio of valiant Virginians was, within his own sphere and according to his own ability, a great man, a noble patriot, and a legendary leader. Thus, history has coined them, respectively, as the Sword, the Pen, and the Trumpet of the American Revolution.

What is so surprising to learn about the triumphant trio is that, among them, Patrick Henry was the recognized leader. It is one thing to capture the imagination of the masses or arouse the passions of the populace; it is quite another thing to earn the reverence of the respected and marshal the loyalty of leaders. Yet this is precisely what Patrick Henry accomplished.[17]

When Patrick Henry died in 1799, he was the most famous man in America, with the exception of George Washington.[18] Thomas Jefferson, speaking of Patrick Henry to Daniel Webster, said, "as our leader he was far above all...in the Revolution...it is not easy to say what we would have done without Patrick Henry."[19]

But Patrick Henry got on the bad side of Thomas Jefferson when he questioned the newly written United States Constitution. Henry was deeply concerned that the rights of the states would be pummeled by the way this Constitution was written. And history has proven Henry to be correct.

Jefferson became embittered towards Henry and set himself to tarnish Henry's fame and deface his place in history.[20] When William Wirt, who was writing a biography of Patrick Henry, contacted Jefferson for his input, it became clear to Wirt that Jefferson had some deep bitterness and resentment toward Henry that polluted his ability to recall the truth accurately.[21]

Interestingly enough, Jefferson did the same thing with John Adams, a man who valued and treasured his friendship. Jefferson, in a document that had wide circulation, "tagged Adams with being both mentally unsound and a monarchist, the two charges most commonly and unjustly made against him for the rest of his life."[22] John Adams, who was to become the second president of the United States, was anything but mentally unsound. Nor did he advocate that America should have a king. But Jefferson attempted to defame Adams, much as he had slandered Patrick Henry.

The tongue and pen of Thomas Jefferson could cut like steel, and it wounded best in the back. Needless to say, Jefferson was not respected for his integrity. But both John Adams and Patrick Henry were known as men of unimpeachable integrity.[23]

DESPISING AND PRIZING

This next verse is one of the strongest in the entire Old Testament and it runs absolutely against the grain of our culture.

> In whose eyes a reprobate is despised,
> But who honors those who fear the LORD;
> He swears to his own hurt and does not change. (v. 4)

Let's take these three concepts in order.

First, the man of integrity despises a reprobate. There is no easing into this one. A reprobate is an immoral person. The *Oxford English Dictionary* defines "reprobate" as one who is "depraved, degraded, morally corrupt; of abandoned character, lost to all sense of religious or moral obligation; rejected by God, lost or hardened in sin."[24]

This ties in directly with verse 5. So, let's jump to that verse very quickly and see the connection:

He does not put out his money at interest,
Nor does he take a bribe against the innocent.
He who does these things will never be shaken.

In Israel you could not lend your money to another Israeli and charge interest. Lending was a family matter, and interest wasn't charged within the family. Verse 5 also condemns bribery against the innocent. God hates these things, and those who love God and live on His holy hill will also hate what God hates. This ties in directly with "despising a reprobate."

The word *despise* is "not so much the emotion of hatred as the deliberate rejection of wicked ways" (see verse 1).[25] Our culture is so far gone that if you refuse to give your approval to homosexual behavior and speak a word against it, you would stand a very good chance of being fired by your company.

Yet on the other hand, the man of integrity, "honors those who fear the LORD." America used to support, by and large, biblical values, but those days are over. If you stand against immorality, and honor those who honor the Lord, you stand a very good chance of paying some very hard consequences.

The majority of men sell out their integrity at this very point. Not long ago, before all the terrorism and mayhem, Mary and I celebrated our wedding anniversary by going to New York. We had a great time seeing the sights and taking in a few Broadway productions. We went to one play that we knew very little about, but we'd heard from some people at the hotel that it was a marvelous comedy. And it *was* funny and very clever…for the first two acts. But in the third act, it broke down very quickly.

A married couple in their fifties was entertaining a childhood friend of the wife. The wife and this other woman were having a great time remembering their days in school together. They hadn't seen each other in years. And then, out of the blue, this very attractive friend mentioned that she would be available to sleep with both of them that night. The married couple was stunned at the idea. But then the girlfriend walked over and kissed the wife. Then she kissed the husband. And within seconds, both husband and wife were considering the idea.

This all happened in less than ninety seconds. In that period of time, we went from a funny and witty comedy to lesbianism. The theatre was full of nice, friendly American citizens from all over the nation. And they were all laughing and applauding. Ten years ago, many of those people would have despised what was on the stage and walked out in protest. But when I grabbed Mary's hand and headed for the aisle, as far as I could tell, we were the only ones to leave.

So what will we be laughing at and accepting ten years from now that we despise today?

I shudder to imagine.

THE HEART OF THE MATTER

In my opinion, one line in verse 4 sets forth the acid test of a man's integrity: *"He swears to his own hurt and does not change."*

This is what separates the men from the boys. What Psalm 15 is teaching here is that if you give your word, either verbally or by signing your name to a contract, and later the circumstances change to actually bring harm to you if you keep your word, the man of God goes ahead and fulfills his pledge. That's what it means to swear to your own hurt. The vast majority of men are willing to keep their word as long as it doesn't *cost* them anything. But some things are more important to them than integrity. Like money.

John Piper writes:

There is a tremendous temptation to break your word when a pledge or a contract turns out to be a financial fiasco. But when Psalm 15 describes the kind of person who "may dwell on God's holy hill," one of the marks of that person is that he "swears to his own hurt and doesn't change."

In other words, he makes a promise, and even if it hurts to follow through on it, he does not go back on his commitment. His word is more valuable than his money. His integrity is more precious than his wealth. He stands by his word even if it hurts.[26]

Then Piper recalls the story of King Amaziah in 2 Chronicles 25:5–9. Amaziah was king of the southern kingdom, Judah. And the nation was threatened by the armies of the Edomites. So Amaziah instituted a national draft to conscript every healthy man over the age of twenty. He came up with 300,000 men.

Still unsure that he had enough men, he went to the Northern Kingdom of Israel and made a deal with Israel to provide 100,000 additional troops for a sum that would equal 6600 pounds of silver.

That might have been a wise military contingency, but there was one small problem with that plan. God was against it. The Lord opposed Israel at this time in their history because of their grievous sin. A prophet of God came to Amaziah and told him that if he went into battle with the 100,000 men of Israel he would lose, because God would not go with them. When Amaziah heard this declaration of the prophet, the very first words out of his mouth were, "But what about the money I paid those guys?"

That's not exactly what he said, but it's a pretty close translation. What he actually said to the prophet was, "But what shall we do for the hundred talents which I have given to the troops of Israel?"

In other words, God doesn't want me to go into battle with those guys. If I go into battle with them, I'll get my tail kicked. I obviously don't want to lose! But—what about the money?!

And then the prophet responded to Amaziah, "The LORD has much more to give to you than this" (2 Chronicles 25:9).

Piper comments: "In other words, 'Trust God and keep your word!' Stand by your commitment because the Lord will take care of you and see that your integrity is rewarded in ways that you can never imagine."

The issue at a moment like this is our trust in God. Will we trust God to act for us? Will we take Psalm 37:5 to heart and bank on it? "Commit your way to the LORD, Trust also in Him, and He will do it." Will we trust God to come through for us in His way and His time?

Human promises are broken because people do not trust God. In fact, they don't even *think* of God. He's not in the equation. Money is in the equation. Shrewdness is in the equation. Human probabilities are in the equation. But God is forgotten. He just doesn't seem as real as the money we might lose.[27]

It was Frank McKinney Hubbard who said, "When a fellow says, 'It ain't the money, it's the principle of the thing,' it's the money."

The money is so often the heart of the matter.

Admittedly, this is a hard issue to get your hands around. Writer Vic Oliver has described the dilemma perfectly:

> If a man runs after money, he's money-mad; if he keeps it, he's a capitalist; if he spends it, he's a playboy; if he doesn't get it, he's a ne'er-do-well; if he doesn't try to get it, he lacks ambition. If he gets it without working for it, he's a parasite; and if he accumulates it after a lifetime of hard work, people call him a fool who never got anything out of life.

Quite frankly, what people think about you and your money isn't worth a plug nickel. What matters is what God thinks. People can't see the heart. God can. God knows if money is more important to us than He is. And He knows if it isn't. God knows when a man loves integrity more than money. Sometimes it's a very subtle and fine line that forces us to choose between the money and our integrity. Sometimes it isn't crystal clear. As a matter of fact, that line between integrity and money can become very obscure. So what do you do in that kind of situation? It really comes down to two possibilities when things are foggy: You could lose your money or you could lose your integrity.

After looking at it from every angle and seeking wisdom to do the right thing, if you're still not sure, then here is what you should do: *Choose to lose the money.*

Wouldn't it be better to err on the side of losing your money rather than losing your integrity? Sure it would. You can afford to lose the money—even if you're dead broke. But integrity, well, that's something you can't afford to lose.

Integrity may not get you the big head. But it will certainly keep you on the Big Hill.

And that's a piece of real estate that's non-negotiable.

EPILOGUE

A PARTING CHALLENGE

Times are bad but God is good.

RICHARD SIBBES

THERE'S AN OLD ROCK SONG THAT CONTAINS THE PHRASE, "Come on, baby, let the good times roll." Everyone wants the good times. Everyone likes the good times. But the good times don't go on forever, do they? They don't just roll and roll without some kind of interruption.

Our national good times were interrupted permanently on the morning of September 11, 2001. As we watched the television images of those passenger planes slamming into the World Trade Center towers (again and again and again), our minds refused to comprehend the reality of it all. We couldn't quite bring ourselves to believe what we were seeing. But way down deep in every American soul, a cold realization began to dawn: The good times had just stopped rolling.

Before September 11 we had more affluence, more freedom, more stuff, more games, more concerts, more movies, more jobs, more self-absorption, more pornography, more Internet, more travel, more news, more cell phones, and more four-dollar cups of coffee than any nation in the history of the world. The good times were *rollin'*.

On the morning of September 10, I was out doing my five-mile walk. As I walk, I pray. And for some reason on that morning, I did something that I don't believe I'd ever done before. I thanked God for a nation at peace. I thanked God that my two sons were not in some remote region of the world fighting an enemy who wanted to spill their blood on that foreign soil. I thanked God that He had been good to us and that we were free from war.

I was teaching a men's study that night, and in the course of the evening, I mentioned my prayer of that morning. I told the guys how thankful I was that we were at peace and not at war.

And the next morning, everything changed.

You already know how much I look forward to reading Peggy Noonan's column each week in the *Wall Street Journal*. In last night's column, she described some of the changes everyone has felt since September 11:

> There are a lot of quiet moments going on. Have you noticed? A lot of quiet transformations, a lot of quiet action and quiet conversations. People are realigning themselves. I know people who are undergoing religious conversions, and changes of faith. And people who are holding on in a new way, and with a harder grip, to what they already have and believe in.
>
> Some people have quietly come to terms with the most soul-chilling thoughts. A young man I know said to me last week…"I have been thinking about the end of the American empire." And I thought, *Oh my boy, do you know the import, the weight, of the words you are saying?* And then I thought: *Yes, he does. He's been thinking, quietly.*
>
> Some people are quietly defining and redefining things. I am one of them. We are trying to define or paint or explain what the old world was, and what the new world is, and how the break between them—the exact spot where the stick broke, cracked, splintered—could possibly have been an hour in early September.[1]

Peggy Noonan is right. Americans have been thinking quietly. We're quietly coming to grips with the fact that we live in a nation at war. The enemy is already here, hidden among us. And we have no idea where or when they will strike next. People have already died from handling mail contaminated with anthrax. Where will these camouflaged enemies hit us tomorrow? Will they taint our water supply or undermine the power grid or fly a plane into a nuclear plant? We don't know what their next move might be. But we know in our hearts that it may get much, much worse in our nation before it gets better.

And the quiet question in everyone's mind is: *How will we ever get through this?* As I began this book, I was aware that some people who would read it would be going through some hard and difficult things in their lives. Things like cancer, divorce, bankruptcy, and layoffs. But going through a war never entered my mind.

Now, that's precisely where we are.

How will we ever get through all of what lies ahead?

ONWARD CHRISTIAN SOLDIERS

We are obviously not the first generation to be at war. For a nation to enjoy peace for as long as we have is very rare in the pages of history.

As believers, we find ourselves engaged in battles on several different fronts. Since the earliest days of Christianity, followers of Christ have waged a war for truth.

Martin Luther found himself right in the middle of it. If Luther had not gone to war, you and I would have severely narrow options for attending church this Sunday. There would be no Lutheran church, Presbyterian church, Baptist church, Bible church, Evangelical Free church, or Pentecostal church.

Your only option would be a Roman Catholic church.

Martin Luther was a Roman Catholic priest obsessed with finding forgiveness for his sins. He would fast for days at a time, confessing every sin he could ever remember committing. And then, emotionally exhausted in his search to find God's grace, he would slump in discouragement, knowing full well he had forgotten some sins from his past, and therefore couldn't find complete forgiveness.

When Luther read the book of Romans and discovered that "the just shall live by faith," he realized that forgiveness was not something that we earned, but something we were given by the completed work of Christ on the cross. That realization changed not only his life, but all of history.

Martin Luther realized he could not keep this truth to himself. He had to preach and proclaim it publicly. And when he nailed his 95 Theses on the door at Wittenberg Castle, the whole world quaked. Why? Because one man had the courage to go into battle against the power, bureaucracy, and political and economic stranglehold of the Roman church.

Because Luther was willing to go into battle and put his life on the line, a Reformation took place that recovered the truth of the gospel from a false and corrupt religious system. He took on the religious, political, and economic powers of his day all by himself. And by God's grace, he got through it.

In Scotland, another Roman Catholic priest by the name of John Knox heard of Luther's discovery and stand. Because Knox discovered the same principle of justification by faith, you and I are Americans today, rather than subjects of the United Kingdom. If Knox had not stood up against Mary, Queen of Scots, who was killing Protestants right and left, there would have been no American revolution.

Knox had the courage to teach that if a king is disobedient to the Word of God, then Christians have the right to refuse obedience, because their first allegiance is to obey the Word of God. No king is above the law, Knox taught. In his day, that was a red-hot radical teaching. It could have easily caused him to be drawn and quartered. But that did not deter Knox from going into battle to declare the truth of the Word of God.

Many of the men and women who stood for the same truths as Luther and Knox gave their lives for the testimony of Jesus. They had the courage to battle to the end for the truth, even if it meant being beheaded, drowned, or buried alive. None of those things deterred God's plan to build steel into their eternal souls.

Not everyone is willing to go into battle and put everything on the line. Douglas Wilson writes:

> A certain type of man is always able to trim his sails to suit the prevailing winds, and he takes pride in the fact that he is adept at it. He does not know where he is going, but he is making good time. Because everything is proceeding so smoothly, he thinks a final reckoning will never come, but it does.[2]

I am assuming in this book that you know where you are going. I am assuming you have given your life to Christ, and that He is your Savior and Lord.

One of the themes in this book has been that men who know where they are going often do *not* make good time. Yes, we know God has saved us through Christ and that ultimately we are going to heaven, but why does God interrupt our plans so often? Why have our dreams and ambitions not been realized? Why have we experienced so many trapdoors that fly open beneath our feet? Why are others who are not following Christ so successful and on schedule? Robert Leighton once commented that "He gives often more of the world to those that shall have no more thereafter." But it is a battle to keep the true perspective that will enable us to get through.

GROUND ZERO FOR THE FAMILY

As I bring this chapter and book to a close, may I mention another battle we are engaged in? It is a battle that has been taking place in America over the last forty or so years.

Last year, retiring United States Senator Daniel Patrick Moynihan was asked to identify the biggest change in his forty-year political career. Moynihan, an erudite intellectual who has served presidents of both parties with distinction, responded: "The biggest change, in my judgment, is that the family structure has come apart all over the North Atlantic world." This momentous transformation, Moynihan added, has occurred in a "historical instant. Something that was not imaginable forty years ago has happened."[3]

It was unimaginable to us on September 10 that the event of the next morning would take place. It was also unimaginable forty years ago that the families of America would be in near-total collapse. But that's exactly where we are. The family in America is hanging together by a worn and torn piece of Scotch tape, frayed at both ends. This battle for marriage is being lost. And most significantly, it's being lost within the church itself. There is as much divorce inside the evangelical church in America as there is outside the church. And the excuses of Christian men who have left their posts know no boundaries.

In his book, *The Broken Hearth,* William Bennett observes:

Compared to a generation ago, American families today are much less stable; marriage is far less central; divorce, out-of-wedlock births, and cohabitation are vastly more common; and children are more vulnerable and neglected, less well-off, and less valued. Public attitudes toward marriage, sexual ethics, and child-rearing have radically altered for the worse. In sum, the family has suffered a blow that has no historical precedent—and one that has enormous ramifications for American society.[4]

Maggie Gallagher has written, "We now live in a society where it is legally easier and less risky to dump a wife than to fire an employee."[5]

We have looked through the lens of the camera time and time again at Ground Zero in New York. We have seen the twisted girders and the brave men who work twelve-hour shifts finding body parts amidst the still-smoldering wreckage.

It is unimaginable. But that's also a picture of what has happened to the family in America. And may I remind you that there are many Christian families who have been lost in the wreckage?

Theodore Roosevelt once said that "the greatest thing a man can ever do is to stay married." The greatest thing a man does is not to get married. Any man can do that. The greatest thing a man does is to *stay* married.

A FINAL CHALLENGE

Everything has changed in America. We are at war.

You had issues in your life before September 11. I imagine that those issues are still with you. And you have been asking yourself, "How in the world will I ever get through this?" And now, on top of everything else, you have a war and an uncertain future to get through.

I want to close this book by issuing a challenge to you.

Are you married? Then stay married.

This is no time to be checking out the new receptionist who works at your office. This is a time to be committed. This is the time to be a man.

Families have always gone through hard times. That has been true for centuries. But in the last forty years, we have developed a new kind of effeminate man. I don't mean a man who has the characteristics and mannerisms of a woman. I'm talking about guys—and in many cases, Christian guys—who take off and abandon their wives and kids when life throws them a few challenges.

Oh yes, their excuses are legion. But the fact of the matter is they cut out when the going got tough.

The middle of a war is no time to walk away from your family just because you and your wife aren't seeing eye to eye or having the sex life you had ten years ago. War is a time to stay together. War is a time to be committed. War is a time to forget the petty differences. War is a time to be a man.

Don't you admire those New York City firefighters who ran *up* the stairs of the flaming towers when everyone else was trying to get down the stairs? Why do we all admire them? Because they didn't run away from their responsibilities. They ran *to* their responsibilities. They ran straight into the heat and danger and terror to save life wherever they could. In John 15:13, Jesus said, "Greater love has no one than this, that one lay down his life for his friends." Those firefighters, for the most part, laid down their lives for people they didn't even know. And for that reason we honor them.

In the first outbreak of war, they sacrificed their lives for others.

Who would have faulted them if they had turned around and ran for their lives? But they didn't do that. They were committed to reaching out to other people who would perish without a helping hand.

Life will probably get harder in the days ahead. That's what happens in wartime. Your family is going to need your help in enduring the heat and pressure of what may lie ahead. Your kids will desperately need you. And so will the grandkids.

So be a man.

Stay married.

Don't abandon your post.

Yield yourself all over again to Christ every day.

And count on this: Whatever's out there, whatever's coming, whatever threatens His redeemed people, He has already defeated.

He will do what it takes to make you strong, but He will never, never leave your side.

You may pass through the heat and fire of a thousand trials, but He will never let go of you. In His strong grip, you will become tempered steel.

Multnomah Publishers

The publisher and author would love to hear your comments about this book. *Please contact us at:*
www.multnomah.net/stevefarrar

STUDY GUIDE

CHAPTER 1
TRAPDOORS AND PIT STOPS

David fell through many a trapdoor in his day and spent a good chunk of his life in pits—some that he dug himself. It's great that someone like him, who is so much like you and me, has gone ahead of us on this path of life and left trail markers.

It's great that he can say words like these in Psalm 55:4–5:

My heart is in anguish within me,
And the terrors of death have fallen upon me.
Fear and trembling come upon me,
And horror has overwhelmed me.

And then turn around in verse 23 of that same psalm and say, "But I will trust in You."

1. Winston Churchill, like David, had many trapdoors open beneath him before he rose to a position of greatness.

    a. What about you? Have you had any "trapdoor transitions" in your life?

    b. What have been the major losses and reversals of your life?

    c. Have you ever felt that these might be the end of you?

2. There were some pretty provocative statements in this chapter. Talk about whether or not you agree with these:

a. "These trapdoors are there by [God's] design and with His permission."

b. "There is a path God has designed ahead of time for you to walk in. He has a plan for you."

3. Every time David was down, he got up again.

a. Have you ever been so low that you were tempted to stay down—maybe even to the point of ending your own life? Talk about that.

b. How do you interpret 1 Corinthians 10:13 in light of those feelings?

4. So far we've been talking about negative transitions, but have you ever experienced a *positive* reversal? What was it?

5. Take a sheet of paper and chart out your life, marking the positive and negative reversals. Does this explain some things about who you are right now?

6. David was anointed to succeed Saul as king, but that succession didn't happen for over a decade.

a. Have you ever felt God calling you to something and yet not allowing you to do it?

b. Why do you think God sometimes inserts a pause between the anointing and the enacting?

7. During the ten to twelve years that Saul was chasing David around the desert, David had several opportunities to take matters into his own hands, kill Saul, and ascend the throne that was rightfully his (see 1 Samuel 24 and 26). But he refused those chances because it was not God's time or God's way.

a. Have you ever had the opportunity to take a shortcut to where you believe God wanted you to eventually be? What was it and what did you do?

b. Was it the right decision?

8. Are you enjoying a season of success right now? Take a moment to thank the Lord for it. But be sure that you're not trusting in that success, for it could be gone tomorrow.

    a. Can you identify a successful area in your life that you might be leaning on too heavily?

    b. What might you do to bring things back into balance?

9. Life can be the pits—literally. Sometimes those pits come on us unexpectedly; other times we dig them for ourselves.

    a. Are you in a pit right now? Do you find yourself saying, "How will I ever get through this?"

    b. Are you now or have you ever been in a pit that you've dug for yourself? Explain.

c. Can you believe that this pit might be unscheduled from your perspective but scheduled from God's?

d. Some people, when they encounter loss or hardship, say that the devil has attacked them. Yet Job said that God was the one who had allowed the reversal to come. Which direction do you tend to lean?

e. Have you ever been in a pit and seen, maybe only in hindsight, that God had sent you there for your good?

f. Joseph, David, and Job all had pit stop experiences yet were mightily used by God. There seems to be a connection between the deepness of the pit and the greatness intended for you by God. Winston Churchill serves as a contemporary example. Can you think of others?

10. Do you agree with the statement in the chapter that the ultimate purpose behind your time in the pit is that you will become more like Christ? Can you see any truth to that in your own life?

CHAPTER 2
THIS IS A TEST

The Bible teaches us that God will conduct a number of unannounced pop quizzes throughout our lives:

The...LORD's...eyelids test the sons of men.
The LORD tests the righteous and the wicked.
(Psalm 11:4–5a)

The Christian life itself is characterized by trials and testing. Unlike our earthly teachers, some of whom we're sure were only out for our misery, our heavenly Teacher tests us so that we will improve our Christlikeness scores. With His help, you can get through.

1. What do you think about Charles Spurgeon's statement that great hearts can only be made through great troubles?

2. The beams in Oxford's New College lasted five centuries before needing to be replaced.

a. When it comes to how you're living the Christian life, do you feel like one of those oak beams—or something closer to particle board?

b. The story about New College says that the man who crafted the beams also provided for their eventual replacement, half a millennium later. Long before the people knew they had a need, the provision had been put in place. How has God worked like that for you?

3. If you're a Christian, you've faced some tough tests in your Christian walk.

a. Name one test that you passed with flying colors.

b. Name one test that you failed.

c. As you look back on both, can you see any evidence of God using them to move you closer to God and godliness?

4. Do you think it's true that "all of the tests in the Christian life are pop quizzes," things you can't study up for? If so, why do you think God does it this way?

5. Did you come to Christ thinking that life would become easier if you followed Him? Is there any sense in which that has proven true? Is there any sense in which it has proven false?

6. Do you think there's anything to the notion that our culture has led us to believe that we're not supposed to suffer at all? In what way does the notion of inevitable suffering fly in the face of our modern culture?

7. Many Christians seem to think that an absence of hardship is a sign of God's love. That they think this way can be proven because when hardship does come, they wonder where God is.

    a. Have you ever gone through a test that made you wonder where God was?

    b. Is there any sense in which the presence of hardship, not its absence, is a sign of God's love?

    c. What do you think hardship tells us about God?

    d. Does Hebrews 5:8 have any bearing on this discussion?

8. As you look back over the tests that you've faced in your life, do you detect a pattern? Does God tend to test you with a certain kind of test—financial, for instance—while He tests someone else with another kind of test? If you can detect such a pattern, what do you think it means?

9. J. I. Packer said, "Suffering is getting what you do not want while wanting what you do not get."

a. Is this a good definition of suffering? How would you change it?

b. If you were completely content with what you have—and without what you do not have—would you still be suffering?

10. If it is true that "God always has a specific goal in mind when He allows us to encounter a pop quiz" and that there is always "something in particular that He wants to test," can you identify what God may be trying to test in your current trials?

11. Here is a statement from the chapter: "Great character is the cumulative result when great pain and great disappointment intersect in a man with a teachable spirit."

a. Do you agree?

b. What would be the result of great pain and disappointment in the life of a man who did not have a teachable spirit?

12. George Mueller said, "Trials, obstacles, difficulties, and sometimes defeats, are the very food of faith."

a. What do you think he meant, and do you agree?

b. Compare this to Paul's statement in 2 Corinthians 12:9–10.

13. Is there a connection between passing character tests and a man's lasting legacy? What is that connection? Name some examples not mentioned in the chapter.

14. Think of this statement from the chapter: "When we respond to God's teaching He withdraws the testing."

a. Have you found that to be true in your own Christian walk?

b. Are you going through a test right now that you could possibly shorten by somehow turning to God in obedience?

c. Why not do so right now?

15.   Abraham Lincoln did not know what great calling God was preparing him for. All he could see were the defeats and personal losses. He might have even been tempted to think that God had it in for him. But in hindsight, we see that God was preparing him for a great work.

a. Are you in the midst of great suffering right now? Are you being tested to the limits of your ability to endure? It probably doesn't feel like God has anything in store for you but more suffering. Can you believe that maybe, just maybe, He's preparing you for a great calling, too?

b. On the other hand, God may simply be taking extra care to chisel you into the image of Jesus Christ. Maybe that's the "great work" He's calling you to. What a privilege that He would take so much care to make you like His beloved Son! Take a moment to praise Him for His love.

CHAPTER 3
ROBINSON CRUSOE

Robinson Crusoe found himself on a desert island without hope of rescue. He called it his prison. Yet something happened to him that caused his perspective to change. He saw that what had seemed so terrible had actually worked out to his good.

"Offer to God a sacrifice of thanksgiving
And pay your vows to the Most High;
Call upon Me in the day of trouble;
I shall rescue you, and you will honor Me."
(Psalm 50:14–15)

1. Tom Hanks' character in *Cast Away* never called on God.
    a. Do you think our society has completely abandoned God?

    b. Is there any evidence to the contrary?

2. God had promised that David would succeed Saul as king. Though many things happened to David that might lead him to doubt that promise, he always believed God would do His part.
    a. Is there a promise of God that you are inclined to doubt right now?

b. Is it hard to hold on to your faith in the midst of crushing hardship?

c. How did David's faith endure his trials?

d. Have you ever gone through a time when what God was doing in your life seemed contrary to what He has promised to do?

e. Can you do as Thomas Watson suggests and "Trust God when providences seem to run quite contrary to promises"?

3. Robinson Crusoe was a prodigal son running from God, his father, and all he knew to be right.

a. Have you ever played the prodigal son?

b. At some point in your flight did you find yourself in a pit?

c. Did it ever occur to you that the pit might be God's merciful intervention in your life?

d. When you were in the pit, did you come to your senses and decide to turn around?

e. If so, take a moment now to worship God for His pursuing love.

4. It is human nature to focus on the negative aspects of our situation. But God's nature is different.

a. If you're like most people, you're probably absorbed with the unpleasantness of your current trial, but can you flip it upside down and identify some mercy in it?

b. Think of the worst situation you've lived through: Has any good arisen from it?

5. Do what Robinson Crusoe did:
    a. Take a piece of paper and draw a line down the middle from top to bottom. Write "evil" atop the left column and "good" atop the right. Start listing the bad stuff—but don't stop there. Go over to the right side of the paper and write out the good, as well. As you do the same exercise that Robinson Crusoe did, you will discover that as bad as that pit may be, it's not all bad.

    b. As you go through your own "evil" column and fill the matching "good" column, is something happening to your attitude? To your faith? Are you finding the oasis in the desert?

6. Robinson Crusoe came to a point of acceptance regarding his situation on the island. With that acceptance came a huge sense of relief and comfort.
    a. Have you ever struggled against something that was going in a direction other than what you wanted, and then finally accepted it?

    b. What did it feel like when you accepted the situation?

7. Do you agree with the following passage from the chapter?
    Do you feel marooned in some nagging, heartbreaking crisis in your life? Then you must reason the same way that Crusoe did. You must come to the point where you can say this: "God allowed me to get into these circumstances for a reason that will somehow shake out for my good. Nothing is bigger than God, and nothing can stop God doing good for me and to me. If God has me in a pit, it's because He's going to somehow work this pit for my good."

8. Chuck Smith said, "Before He could work through me, He had to work in me."

    a. Look up Philippians 2:12–13. What does this passage say about God's activity in our lives?

    b. Have you seen evidence of this same dynamic in your life?

    c. What work is God doing in you now?

9. Do you think it's true that there is no level ground for a Christian in his relationship to God, that he's either advancing or declining? Which are you doing now?

10. What does this mean: "Some providences, like Hebrew letters, must be read backwards"? Have you found it to be true? Give an example.

11. Do you agree that God's provision is always exactly on time? Can you cite an example? Take a moment to praise the God of perfect timing.

12. Respond to this passage from the chapter: "Somewhere in that tattered, fraying coat of circumstance is a check made out to you that is drawn on the Bank of the Goodness of God. How much is it for? I don't know the amount, but it's bigger than what you lost. Much bigger."

13. When Robinson Crusoe read the Bible he discovered Jesus Christ—and gave his heart fully to Him. Have you done the same? If not, or if you're not sure, someone in your group would love to talk to you about it.

CHAPTER 4
THE BATTLE OF ALL BATTLES

Sometimes it feels like God has forsaken us—or worse, that He's actively against us. We run toward an open door and—*wham!*—it's slammed in our faces. We hold out hope that this job interview may be the one that saves our family from poverty, but—*boom!*—the job is given to someone else. We're just trying to get by and then—*slam!*—someone we love is diagnosed with a terminal disease.

All of these things are out of our control. But they're under God's control—so why aren't they working out right? Doesn't He love us? Doesn't He have the power to make it work out for our good? What's going on?

Will the Lord reject forever?
And will He never be favorable again?
Has His lovingkindness ceased forever?
Has His promise come to an end forever?
Has God forgotten to be gracious,
Or has He in anger withdrawn His compassion? Selah.
(Psalm 77:7–9)

1.   Sometimes we all get to the place where we feel like God's not living up to His side of the Christian life bargain.

a. Have you ever felt that God was actually working against you?

b. Has time given you the benefit of hindsight so that maybe you understand a little of why He did what He did?

2.   When Josh was on the bottom of the pool, I cried out to my brother. I knew he would hear me, I knew he would hear the distress in my voice, and I knew he would come.

   a. Have you ever cried out to someone that way?

   b. Have you ever cried out to God that way?

   c. Have you ever wondered if God was even there to hear you call?

3.   Compare Psalm 77 with Psalm 22.

4.   Respond to the following passage from the chapter:
   The battle to connect with God when everything is falling apart in your life is the most exhausting and trying conflict you will ever experience. And what makes it so hard is that God is supposed to be there for you when the walls close in on your life! He's supposed to be there when the trapdoor opens beneath your feet and you find yourself in that dark, loathsome pit. But He is nowhere to be found.

5. J. C. Penney suffered the loss of his first wife, his second wife, and then his fortune. Sitting in his sanatorium room, he heard a hymn being sung by the staff. "God used that bit of verse to reconnect his heart to the Lord he thought had abandoned him."

    a. Have you ever felt that the sorrows in your life would crush you?

    b. Have you ever felt that God had abandoned you? Are you feeling that way now?

    c. Has God ever used something unexpected—a song, a greeting card, a snatch of overheard conversation—to break through and bring you hope? Give an example.

6. It was said of John Adams that he saw "large things largely."
    a. What do you think that means?

    b. Do you agree with this statement: "When we do not understand God's dealings with us, we must attempt to see large things largely"?

c. Think of something large that's happening in your life right now. Now ask God to help you see it largely.

7.   Do you agree that one of the great battles of the Christian life is to fight off wrong thinking about God when His ways don't make sense to us? Can you give an example of wrong thoughts you've had about God?

8.   When a ministry I'd given my all to died, I was very angry with God. But later I saw that He had something better in mind for me, and I found myself praising God that He had let my plan die.

   a. Have you ever suffered a disappointment only to later realize that it was the best thing possible?

   b. Have you ever found yourself shaking your fist at God for doing what you later found out was for your benefit?

9.   When God is apparently inactive in the present, we must remember what He has done in the past.

   a. Take out a sheet of paper and chart out for yourself the times you have seen God work on your behalf in your life.

b. What does it do to your attitude to see God's intervention in your life?

c. Read Psalm 78. It is a catalog of God's works for Israel. God's people rehearsed those great events when they needed to hold on to faith. You can use your own sheet to do the same.

10. React to these sentences from the chapter:
a. "God will go to any extreme to direct, guide, and protect His people."

b. "He will do it on His timetable, not mine."

11. Winston Churchill's statue stands with one foot on British soil and one on American soil. In the same way we must stand with one foot in the present, fighting wrong thoughts from Satan, and one foot in the past, remembering God's great works on our behalf.
a. Have you been guilty of having a selective memory regarding the past? Have you remembered the negatives and forgotten the positives?

b. Take a moment now to remember God's good works for you and to praise Him for them.

CHAPTER 5
CAREER INTERRUPTIONS

If God is for us, who can be against us? If God wants you in a certain job, pity the one who tries to keep you from it. But if God wants to test you by laying you off, who can prevent Him from doing His will?

The question, then, becomes whether you and I can hold on in faith until we see Him move again on our behalf.

I waited patiently for the LORD;
And He inclined to me and heard my cry.
He brought me up out of the pit of destruction, out of the miry clay,
And He set my feet upon a rock making my footsteps firm.
(Psalm 40:1–2)

1. In the chapter I say that if you don't know Christ, or if you do know Him but you're lax in your personal application of the truth, your future doesn't look too promising.

    a. Do you agree with me?

    b. Do you know Christ as your Lord and Savior?

    c. Are there any ways in which you have been "lax in your personal application of the truth"?

2. If you're like most men you'll find yourself out of work at some point in your life.

    a. Have you ever been laid off from a job?

    b. Did you feel a drop in your self-esteem, self-worth, and/or self-respect?

    c. Did anything help?

    d. How did you finally recover—or have you?

3. There is a voice in American culture that encourages us to consistently and purposefully choose career and business over personal relationships.

    a. Have you felt the tug of this voice?

    b. Have you ever given in to it, to the detriment of your relationships?

c. What have you found that helps?

4. Do you think Hershey is right when he says our culture tells us: "If you're living life right, you're in ecstasy most of the time"? How would you say it differently?

5. If you've been out of work for an extended time, you know all about excess free time. You've pulled all your strings and called in all your favors, but now you're left staring at daytime soaps and talk shows.
    a. How do you stave off depression?

    b. How do you maintain a positive sense of self-esteem?

    c. What if these weeks of unemployment turn into months? What if they turn into years?

6. In a sense, writer Peggy Noonan anticipated the September 11 terrorist attacks when she said that our time of affluence in the late 1990s was our last big moment of pleasure before something terrible happened.

a. Does this strike a chord in you? Explain.

b. Do you sense a spiritual significance to the lull before the storm?

c. If so, what do you think that significance might be?

7. Thousands of people lost their lives or their loved ones in that terrorist attack. Many tens of thousands more lost their jobs as a result.

a. Are you in either group?

b. Though you may have lost your job as a direct or indirect result of that attack, have you stopped lately to thank God that you did not lose your life or a loved one in it?

c. Why not do so now?

8. Robert E. Lee had to turn down the opportunity of a lifetime. He had to die to the dreams of his heart and career for the greater good.

a. Have you ever been in Lee's shoes? Have you ever had to let a dream die for the greater good? What was it?

b. Have you ever laid a dream down only to find it resurrected and given back to you later?

c. What do you think this tells us about God?

9. Sometimes God makes us wait. But of course, we hate waiting. Still, His ways and His timing are always worth waiting for.

a. Can you think of an example of when waiting on God proved to be worth the wait?

b. Can you think of an example when someone tried to seize a dream before God's time for it had come? Did it work out well?

c. Read and meditate on Isaiah 40:30–31.

CHAPTER 6
CAREER INTERRUPTIONS, PART 2

While we live here on earth, we're led to believe that achievement in our chosen career is the definition of success. But in God's eyes, you're successful when you look more and more like His Son.

For neither from the east nor from the west nor from the desert does promotion come;

But God is the Judge. He puts down one and promotes another. (Psalm 75: 7, MLB)

1. God used a major career interruption to make Joshua ready to take over for Moses.

   a. If you've had a major career interruption in your life, can you believe that it might be something God is doing to make you ready for greatness?

   b. Looking back over how God has moved in your life, do you have some idea of what kind of work He might be preparing you for now?

2. In your career, do you feel like Moses in the elevator whose cable has snapped or like Joshua in the elevator stuck between floors?

3. I say in the chapter that God's method is to test a man before He uses a man.

    a. Do you agree?

    b. Can you think of examples of this sequence in your own life?

    c. Reflect on Job's words in Job 23:8–12. What nuggets of truth can you take away from these verses in your present circumstances?

    d. What do you think I mean when I say in this chapter that character development comes before ministry?

4. If you are unemployed, you probably just want a job, any job, that will allow you to provide for your family. That's an understandable desire.

    a So how can I say that God may be more interested in doing a work in you than in getting you a job?

b. What does 1 Peter 1:7 indicate is more precious to God than gold?

c. What light does that shine on your unemployment?

5. Joshua and Caleb stood alone against the other ten spies. They had the courage to believe in God's promise despite how things appeared.

a. Have you ever had to face the test of standing alone for God?

b. How did you do?

c. If this test is really measuring who you care about pleasing—God or men—what do you have to conclude about yourself?

6. I challenge you in the chapter with these words: "When you write up your résumé or go to an interview, tell the truth. Don't hedge the truth and don't pad the facts. You don't have to do that to gain employment. God is your employer. And He is watching to see what you will do under the pressure of a prolonged pit."

a. Have you ever been tempted to hedge the truth in an interview situation?

b. Have you ever told the truth and then been passed over for the job?

c. Did it make you want to fudge a little next time?

d. Remember, when God wants you employed, no person or group is going to be able to stand in the way of you getting that job. Praise Him now for His sovereignty over your employment status. Hold on to the faith that He will reward you for your truthfulness.

7. The second character test that you must face before God really uses you is the test of deep disappointment.

a. Have you ever suffered a disappointment this deep?

b. Have you ever been hurt by someone else's sin?

c. If so, how have you managed the bitterness and resentment over it?

d. Do you think it is true that every morning you have to make the decision whether to live that day in bitterness or to trust God with your life?

8. Deep disappointment can gnaw at you under the surface, carving out a reservoir of hatred that one day might erupt.

a. Reflect on Hebrews 12:15. What "root of bitterness" do you need to deal with before it consumes you—and defiles others?

b. Can you follow Robert E. Lee's advice to "cut it down and forget it"?

9. The third test is to believe in the perfection of God's timing.

a. Can you attest to the idea that sometimes God's timing seems way off? Name an example.

b. Does it feel like life is passing you by as you sit here in neutral?

c. Can you think of any examples that bear out this statement: "If you stay faithful, at the right time He will reward your faithfulness"?

10. What do you think of the image of the moth escaping the cocoon? Can you identify anything in your own life that feels like a struggle that may actually be strengthening you for what lies ahead?

11. Comment on this statement from the chapter: "Spiritual maturity never comes in a package with microwave instructions. That's because spiritual maturity can only be produced in Crock-Pots."

12. How does Hebrews 11:32–40 support the idea that some people will be promoted but others will not?

CHAPTER 7
TOTALED OUT

Depression can threaten to wipe us out. It's not just the loss of a job that can force men against the ropes, but it's usually a loss of some kind. Sometimes it can make us think that there's no way on earth we'll endure the heat of our tests and trials.

In the day of my trouble I sought the Lord;
In the night my hand was stretched out without weariness;
My soul refused to be comforted.
(Psalm 77:2)

1.   If you're in some kind of pit, do you feel pretty much alone? Would it help to find someone who had been in that same pit and lived to tell the tale?

2.   How would you rate yourself right now on the three scales:
     a. Physical?

     b. Spiritual?

     c. Emotional?

3. Have you ever gotten ahead of the Shepherd instead of waiting on the Shepherd to lead? Describe such an episode in your life.

4. When Mary was in the hospital, I was tempted to accept a position at a church just because they had said yes to me. But then I felt I was about to make the wrong decision: "I was already in hot water, but taking a church just because it would solve our financial woes was just asking for boiling water."

a. Have you ever been tempted to take a job, even if it's completely wrong for you—just to get some money coming in?

b. Have you ever taken such a job and lived to regret it?

c. Have you ever refused such a job and then been glad you didn't take it?

5. Many men who lose their jobs and find themselves continually unable to get a new one may stumble into deep depression.

a. Do you think you are or have ever been there?

b. Are you reaching your personal stress limit?

c. What have you found to be helpful in coping?

6. Do you know personally what I mean about walking on the razor's edge of an emotional breakdown?

7. The bottom line of my friend's despair was that he believed God had abandoned him. Is that where you are right now?

8. Depression, more than any other emotion, drives us to the Psalms. See if these psalms help you give voice to your feelings of hopelessness: Psalm 13, 22, 28, 55, 60, 69, 74, 88, 102, 141.

9. Has your situation caused you to think some wild thoughts about God? Name a few of those.

CHAPTER 8
TOTALED OUT, PART 2

God has a purpose for your suffering. If you're wise, you won't be so upset by the pit that you miss out on the lessons learned there. And one day, you will find yourself qualified to speak to a person in a deep pit much like your own. When God rescues you from the pit, be ready to praise His name to someone else.

But You, O LORD, be not far off;
O You my help, hasten to my assistance.
Deliver my soul from the sword,
My only life from the power of the dog.
Save me from the lion's mouth;
From the horns of the wild oxen You answer me.
I will tell of Your name to my brethren;
In the midst of the assembly I will praise You.
(Psalm 22:19–22)

1. This was my situation all those years ago: Unemployed for nine months, hospital bills skyrocketing, Mary in a high-risk pregnancy, me with meningitis, and then the prospect that our baby would be terribly deformed.

a. Do I have authority to speak to men about being in the pit?

b. Does it lighten your load at all to know that I've been on the ash heap, too?

2.   I prayed two things during that time. See if they resonate with you. If so, make them your prayers, too.

a. Lord, please let me learn everything you have for me in this experience so that I don't have to go through it again!

b. Lord, please take my difficulty and somehow use it to minister to others.

3.   Do you agree with Edith Schaeffer that: "There is always a cost to being used mightily for the Lord"?

4.   Do you agree that the thing that equips you for ministry is not a theological degree, but suffering? By that definition, are you equipped for ministry?

5.   Have you ever asked God to really pick you up and use you as a tool for His kingdom purposes?

a. If so, that should help explain why you find yourself in the midst of a crushing experience: God is equipping you to minister to someone else at a future time.

b. If you have prayed this kind of prayer, do you now find yourself in suffering?

c. If you've never prayed this kind of prayer, would you dare to do so right now?

6. What do I mean by this statement from the chapter: "If you are crushed, if you are depressed, if you are broken, you should know this: All God is doing is answering your prayer"?

7. Read 2 Corinthians 2:3–7. Talk about a time when someone listened to your counsel because you could tell them about a hard time you'd been through in your own life—and about the consolation you received from the "God of all comfort."

8. Depression can make us lose our perspective. We can begin to believe that God has forgotten us. "Sometimes we're so caught up with the conflict within us and around us that we don't even realize that God is being faithful. The reason we don't realize it is because His faithfulness isn't readily apparent. But that doesn't mean it isn't there."

a. Can you testify to that?

b. Talk about a time that was difficult while you were living through it but that later became clear was an act of God's faithfulness.

c. Take a moment right now to praise God for His faithfulness, even though you're praying from the depths of a pit.

CHAPTER 9
GETTING THE BIG HEAD

Four men got "the big head" when images of their faces were carved into Mount Rushmore. It was a great honor reserved for some of the most admired and admirable men in American history.

Many other men have been allowed onto "the big hill" of God. The principal quality of these men, according to Psalm 15, is integrity.

O LORD, who may abide in Your tent?
Who may dwell on Your holy hill?
He who walks with integrity.
(Psalm 15:1–2a)

1.   President Theodore Roosevelt said, "My success so far has only been won by absolute indifference to my future career." He had no interest in winning a future election if it meant that he must sacrifice truth and doing the right thing.

a. Have you ever been in a situation in which you felt as if you were choosing between your future and your integrity?

b. This world does a good job of making the right thing feel like the wrong thing, and vice versa. What are some examples of this?

c. Have you ever done the right thing and then had people—even Christians—try to convince you that it was the wrong thing?

2.   In some men there is a match between what they say and what they do, and in others, there is not.

    a. Benjamin Rush spoke out against slavery yet owned a slave. Robert E. Lee, too, spoke out against slavery—then he freed his inherited slaves and gave them vocational training so they could support themselves and their families.

    b. There was a match between Lee's words and his actions. Is there a match between your words and your actions?

    c. Can you think of any area in which you've been living a double life, appearing to stand for one thing but secretly standing for another?

    d. If so, why not open your heart to allow God to bring your actions and words into line?

3.   Only God's family may dwell on His holy hill. Are you part of God's family? Read 2 Corinthians 13:5 and Romans 8:16.

4. Psalm 15:4 says that the man of integrity despises a reprobate.
   a. What does this mean?

   b. How does this contradict what our culture teaches?

   c. Can this idea be taken too far?

   d. What might be a balanced implementation of this idea?

5. The man of integrity honors those who fear the Lord.
   a. What opportunities have come your way to honor those who fear the Lord?

   b. How does this idea collide with the teachings of our culture?

6. When was the last time you walked out of a theater or turned off a movie as a protest against its content? Should you maybe have walked out, but didn't?

7. If average Americans can applaud lesbianism on stage today, when ten years ago it would have sickened them, what do you think average Americans will be applauding ten years from now?

8. Comment on this statement from the chapter: "The vast majority of men are willing to keep their word as long as it doesn't cost them anything."

9. A man who may dwell on God's holy hill "swears to his own hurt and doesn't change." The idea is that he will stand by his commitments whatever it may cost him.

    a. Are there some commitments you've made that you have considered breaking?

    b. Have you ever stood by a commitment though it cost you dearly?

    c. If so, do you believe you did the right thing?

d. Have you ever sensed God rewarding you for making that stand?

e. Do you agree with me that "the issue at a moment like this is our trust in God. Will we trust God to act for us?"

10. Have you ever been faced with a decision in which you could lose your money or you could lose your integrity? Which did you choose? Was it the right decision?

11. Comment on this statement from the chapter: "Integrity may not get you the big head. But it will certainly keep you on the Big Hill."

NOTES

INTRODUCTION

1. *The World Book Encyclopedia*, Volume 9, p. 3889d.

2. Ibid., p. 3889e.

3. Ibid., p. 3889f.

4. Ibid., p. 3889h.

CHAPTER 1

1. Wendy Elliman "Jerusalem's King David Hotel—fit for a king," *Edmonton Jewish Life*. http://www.compcocity.com/ejl/april/kingdavidh.htm.

2. William Manchester, *The Last Lion: Winston Spencer Churchill* (New York: Dell Publishing, 1983), 880.

3. Bruce H. Wilkinson and Larry Libby, *Talk Thru Bible Personalities* (Atlanta, Ga.: Walk Thru the Bible Ministries, 1983), 84.

4. Ibid., 84.

5. Thomas Watson, *All Things for Good* (Carlisle, Penn.: Banner of Truth Trust, 1663), 25.

6. Ibid., 25.

CHAPTER 2

1. Max Lucado, *The Inspirational Study Bible* (Dallas, Tex.: Word, 1993), 323.

2. Bruce H. Wilkinson and Larry Libby, *Talk Thru Bible Personalities* (Atlanta, Ga.: Walk Thru the Bible Ministries, 1983), 79.

3. Landon Jones, cited by Gary R. Collins and Timothy E. Clinton, *Baby Boomer Blues* (Dallas, Tex.: Word, 1992), 14.

4. Ibid., 3.

5. D. Martyn Lloyd-Jones, *Spiritual Depression* (Grand Rapids, Mich.: Eerdmans, 1965), 224.

6. Fritz Reinecker and Cleon Rogers, *Linguistic Key to the Greek New Testament* (Grand Rapids, Mich.: Regency, 1976).

7. Lloyd-Jones, *Spiritual Depression,* 223.

8. Warren Wiersbe, *Wiersbe's Expository Outlines of the New Testament* (Wheaton, Ill.: Victor, 1992), 720.

9. *Leadership Journal* 4, no. 1 (Winter 1983): p. 83.

10. George Mueller, quoted by Miles J. Stanford, *Principles of Spiritual Growth* (Lincoln, Nebr.: Back to the Bible, 1984), 9.

11. I am indebted to John Piper for this illustration from the life of George Mueller; see John Piper, *The Pleasures of God* (Portland, Ore.: Multnomah, 1991), 190.

12. Lloyd-Jones, *Spiritual Depression,* 230.

13. Piper, *The Pleasures of God,* 189.

14. Roy L. Laurin, *Life Endures* (Grand Rapids, Mich.: Zondervan, 1946), 110.

15. As quoted by David Wilkerson, "The Towers Have Fallen and We Have Missed the Message," *Times Square Church.* http://www.timessquarechurch.org.wtc/010916-1.html. Sermon of September 16, 2001.

CHAPTER 3

1. *The Complete Word Study Old Testament,* ed. Warren Baker et al. (Chattanooga, Tenn.: AMG Publishers, 1994), 2308.

2. John Flavel, *The Mystery of Providence* (Carlisle, Penn.: The Banner of Truth Trust, 1678), 18.

3. Ibid., 18.

4. Ibid., 19–20.

5. Ibid., 49.

6. Thomas Watson, cited by I. D. E. Thomas, *A Puritan Golden Treasury* (Carlisle, Penn.: The Banner of Truth Trust, 1975), 230.

7. Daniel Defoe, *Robinson Crusoe* (New York: Barnes & Noble Books, 1996), 47–8.

8. Ibid., 65.

9. Ibid., 67–8.

10. Ibid., 68.

11. Ibid., 229.

12. Chuck Smith, *Harvest* (Old Tappan, NJ: Chosen, 1987), 28, 40.

13. Bruce H. Wilkinson and Larry Libby, *Talk Thru Bible Personalities* (Atlanta, Ga.: Walk Thru the Bible Ministries, 1983), 85.

14. Stephen Mansfield, *Forgotten Founding Father: The Heroic Legacy of George Whitefield* (Nashville, Tenn.: Cumberland House)

CHAPTER 4

1. David McCullough, *Brave Companions: Portraits in History* (New York: Touchstone Books, 1992), 80.

2. Here are two more reviews, and the reason I include them is to let you know that this is not a wacko, out-of-left-field theory. At least, he convinced *Publisher's Weekly* (not Publisher's Clearing House), a highly respected journal in the publishing world. Here's what their critical reviewer had to say:

> Stinnett provides overwhelming evidence that FDR and his top advisers knew that Japanese warships were heading towards Hawaii. The heart of his argument is even more inflammatory: Stinnett argues that FDR, who desired to sway public opinion in support of U.S. entry in World War II, instigated a policy intended to provoke a Japanese attack.

Finally, Rupert Corwell, in *The London Independent:*

> Robert Stinnett has come as close as any mortal will to proving not only that the president has a pretty shrewd idea the Japanese planned to attack but that he did everything in his power, short of declaring war, to make sure they would...the case put together by Stinnett during thirteen years of research and the Freedom of Information Act, and interviews with participants, is more than persuasive.

3. Robert Stinnett, "December 7, 1941: A Setup from the Beginning," *The Independent Institute,* 7 December 2000. http://independent.org/tii/news/001207Stinnett.html.

4. Ibid.

5. Robert Stinnett, *Day of Deceit: The Truth about FDR and Pearl Harbor* (New York: Touchstone, 2000), xiv.

6. Robert Stinnett, "Pearl Harbor: Official Lies in an American War Tragedy?" *The Independent Institute,* 24 May 2000. http://www.independent.org/tii/forums/000524ipfTrans.html. Transcript from the Independent Policy Forum.

7. Here's an interesting note. After Stinnett's book first came out in hardback, he found an additional four thousand intelligence communication documents under the Freedom of Information Act that further substantiated that the United States government knew in advance that Japan was going to attack Pearl Harbor.

8. Warren Lewis, cited by Douglas Wilson, *For Kirk and Covenant* (Nashville, Tenn.: Cumberland House, 2000), 33.

9. Ibid., 33–4.

10. Ibid., 34.

11. John Woodbridge, *More Than Conquerors* (Chicago: Moody Press, 1992), 342.

12. David McCullough, *John Adams* (New York: Simon & Schuster, 2001), 99.

13. Ibid., 62.

14. C. H. Spurgeon, *The Treasury of David, Volume II* (Byron Center, Mich.: Associated Publishers and Authors, Inc., 1970), 448.

CHAPTER 5

1. Peggy Noonan, "There Is No Time, There Will Be Time," *Wall Street Journal,* http://www.opinionjournal.com/columnists/pnoonan/?id=95001157 .

2. Michael Granberry, "Plano 75093: Trouble in Paradise?" *Dallas Morning News,* 3 September 2001.

3. Terry Hershey, *Young Adult Ministry* (Loveland, Colo.: Group Publishing, Incorporated, 1986) 39.

4. Ibid.

5. Anthony Campolo, *The Success Fantasy* (Colorado Springs, Colo.: Chariot Victor Publishing, 1993)

6. H. W. Crocker III, *Robert E. Lee on Leadership* (Rocklin, Calif.: Forum, 1999), 39.

7. J. Steven Wilkins, *Call of Duty: The Sterling Nobility of Robert E. Lee* (Nashville, Tenn.: Cumberland House Publishing, 1997), 74.

8. Ibid., 80.

9. Ibid., 86–7.

10. Ibid., 83.

CHAPTER 6

1. Quoted by Daniel Eisenberg, "Wartime Recession?" *Time,* October 1, 2001, p. 84.

2. *The New Encyclopedia of Christian Quotations,* Compiled by Mark Water (Grand Rapids, Mich.: Baker Book House, 2000), 1131.

3. John Gardner, *On Leadership* (New York: The Free Press, 1990), 114.

4. Charles Colson, *Against the Night* (Ann Arbor: Servant, 1989), 103.

5. Michael Green, *Illustrations for Biblical Preaching* (Grand Rapids, Mich.: Baker, 1989), 326.

6. Ibid., 302.

7. Ibid., 384.

8. *Leadership*, Spring Quarter 1984, p. 45.

CHAPTER 7

1. Matthys Levy and Mario Salvadori, *Why Buildings Fall Down* (New York: Norton, 1992), 223.

CHAPTER 8

1. Edith Schaeffer, *The Tapestry* (Waco, Tex.: Word, 1981), 272.

2. Cited in *Leadership* 4, no. 2 (Spring 1983): p. 93.

CHAPTER 9

1. George Grant, *Carry a Big Stick* (Nashville, Tenn.: Cumberland House, 1996), 11.

2. Ibid.

3. Ibid., 92.

4. Ibid., 12.

5. Ibid., 126.

6. Ibid., 143.

7. Ibid., 191.

8. Ibid., 191–2.

9. Ibid., 142.

10. Ibid., 144.

11. David McCullough, *John Adams* (New York: Simon and Schuster, 2001), 132.

12. Ibid., 132.

13. Ibid., 133.

14. H. W. Crockett, *Robert E. Lee on Leadership* (Rocklin, Cal.: Forum Publishing, 1999), 22.

15. Ibid., 23.

16. C. H. Spurgeon, *The Treasury of David* (Byron Center, Mich.: Associated Publishers and Authors, Inc., 1869), 198.

17. David J. Vaughan, *Give Me Liberty: The Uncompromising Statesmanship of Patrick Henry* (Nashville, Tenn.: Cumberland House Publishing, 1997), introduction.

18. Ibid., 272.

19. Ibid., 18.

20. Ibid., 273.

21. Ibid.

22. McCullough, 433.

23. As I write these words, David McCullough's biography of John Adams is number one on the *New York Times* bestseller list for nonfiction. It seems like everyone is reading this massive biography of a forgotten president. And the question is why? David Gergen offers a possible answer:

> But for all of his mastery at storytelling, McCullough knows that the Adams biography has tapped into something deeper in the American psyche, a longing. One suspects that many of us feel that in public life today, we are losing our moorings, that we are living in smaller times, surrounded too often by smaller men. So, we are

searching our past, returning to the founders, and to others who renew our understanding of what it means to be an American, and to cause us to thrill once again at the journey we have taken as a people. Is it any coincidence that a history by Joseph Ellis, *The Founding Brothers,* is also on the bestseller list these days?

McCullough set out to write a dual biography of Adams and Jefferson—in today's White House parlance, No. 2 and No. 3. But he soon fell out of love with No. 3 (the man who sat out most of the Revolution in Monticello). Instead, he was smitten by No. 2, along with his wife, Abigail. What emerges is a portrait of a loving couple noble to their core. Adams has flaws—as do every one of his compatriots. But he is the only founder who chose on principle not to own slaves, and he answers every call to service, even when it puts his reputation and life in danger.

McCullough was going to write about Thomas Jefferson and John Adams. But the character of Jefferson repelled him and the integrity of John Adams drew him like a magnet.

Did you note that Gergen referred to another bestselling book, *The Founding Brothers*? This book is also about the founding fathers, and there are two drums I must pound right here at this point.

The first is the title *The Founding Brothers*. Have you ever heard that term before when applied to the men who signed the Declaration of Independence? Of course you haven't. The term that has been used for over two hundred years is Founding Fathers. So what is this Founding Brothers stuff? The term "Founding Fathers" is no longer acceptable because it is not politically correct. From now on, these men should be referred to as simply, "The Founders." Another option is "The Founding Brothers" as author Joseph Ellis has titled his book about the Founding Fathers.

You see, the term *fathers* is not acceptable in our culture. Fathers are out of vogue, they are inconvenient and they definitely are not necessary. Not only is our nation becoming a nation where fathers are absent from the home, but we are now trying to delete fathers from our history. I couldn't let that one go by. And by the way, this is an integrity issue. Good families are built on fathers and so are good nations. This renaming of the Founding Fathers is another example of the nonsense that never fails to come from the distorted and darkened minds and foolish pens of the academic and liberal Canaanites that surround us.

But one other drum must be pounded. And it has reference to our discussion about integrity. Joseph Ellis, the author of *Founding Brothers,* is the Ford Foundation Professor of History at Mount Holyoke College. He received the Pulitzer Prize for *Founding Brothers* in 2001. In 1997 he received the National Book Award for *American Sphinx: The Character of Thomas Jefferson.* He is also the author of *Passionate Sage: The Character and Legacy of John Adams.*

His books on Jefferson and Adams examine the character of each man. Yet in June of 2001, it was reported that Ellis, who for years has kept his students and fellow faculty members mesmerized with stories of his service and hair-raising adventures in Viet Nam, never served in Viet Nam. Ellis, a respected historian who makes his living writing on the character and integrity of past American presidents, admitted that he has lied for years about his military service in Viet Nam.

So much for character. So much for integrity.

24. *The Compact Edition of the Oxford English Dictionary,* Volume II (Oxford, England: Oxford University Press, 1971), 2500.

25. Ibid., 658.

26. John Piper, *A Godward Life* (Sisters, Ore.: Multnomah Books, 1997), 94.

27. Ibid., 94.

EPILOGUE

1. Peggy Noonan, "His Delicious, Mansard-Roofed World," *Wall Street Journal,* 26 October 2001. http://www.opinionjournal.com/forms/printThis.html?id=95001382 .

2. Douglas Wilson, *For Kirk and Covenant* (Nashville, Tenn.: Cumberland House, 2000), 170.

3. As quoted by William Bennett, *The Broken Hearth* (New York: Doubleday, 2001), 1.

4. Ibid., 1.

5. Ibid., 29.

We may be in the dark, but we're not alone…

ISBN 1-57673-742-X

A PASSAGE THROUGH THE PSALMS…

GETTIN' THERE

HOW A MAN FINDS HIS WAY ON THE TRAIL OF LIFE

STEVE FARRAR

"When you boil it all down, this is what you've got. You can live a wasted life. Or you can live a wise life. And it all comes down to which trail you choose….You're on a trail right now, at this very instant. You're smack dab in the middle of it. It's a trail of life that begins at birth and ends at death. And right now you're about to take the next step. Only eternity may reveal how crucial that step might be… Let's face it, we've never been down this trail before. We don't have a clue what's around the next bend. Every season of life has its own challenges and gauntlets. We may be in the dark, but we're not alone. The trail has been marked!"

—Steve Farrar

The Measure of a Man

Instruction and motivation from bestselling author Steve Farrar

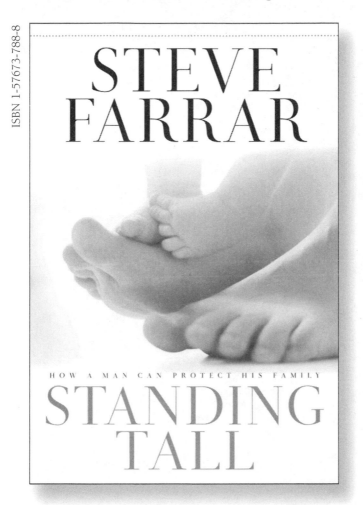

ISBN 1-57673-788-8

In a nation marked by increasing moral decay and spiritual deterioration, men who want to protect their families must not only know their convictions—they must put them into action. Since 1990, over 225,000 men have turned to Steve Farrar's bestselling *Point Man* for advice on leading their families in today's culture. Now, Farrar teaches those same men how to protect their families by asking and responding to difficult questions such as:

- What are the dangers my family faces in the world today?
- How can I take a stand that will protect them?
- What can I do to instill strong convictions in my children?

More than ever before, families and communities need Christian men with discernment and direction. So, discover how you can courageously lead and protect your family by *Standing Tall* in the world today!

Solid Leadership Strategies from the Greatest Commander of All

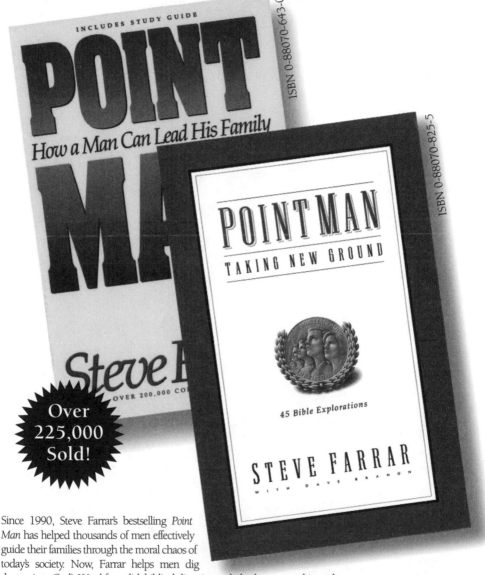

ISBN 0-88070-643-0

ISBN 0-88070-825-5

Over 225,000 Sold!

Since 1990, Steve Farrar's bestselling *Point Man* has helped thousands of men effectively guide their families through the moral chaos of today's society. Now, Farrar helps men dig deeper into God's Word for solid, biblical direction to help them meet this goal.

Building upon the crucial topics introduced in *Point Man*, Farrar's *Point Man: Taking New Ground* explores God's teachings about the subjects most important to husbands and fathers today. Each of these forty-five easy-to-complete readings includes:

- **Daily scripture and devotional passages**
- **Key Bible verses**
- **Practical, personal applications**
- **Daily prayers, and more!**

"Run so that you may obtain the prize."
I Corinthians 9:24

ISBN 1-57673-726-8

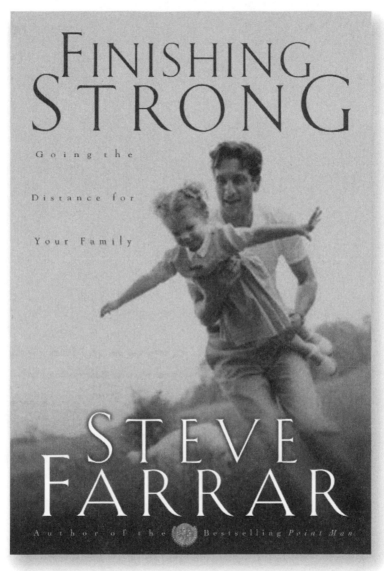

Every day, men see husbands and fathers around them falling to temptations such as workaholism, infidelity, uncontrolled anger, and ethical shortcuts. No man wants to hurt his wife and children. But if he is to "finish strong," living righteously and ethically to the end of his life, he must proactively implement the commitments he has made to Jesus Christ and to his family. In *Finishing Strong*, bestselling men's author Steve Farrar shows husbands and dads how they can do exactly that, teaching them how to recognize and avoid the pitfalls that can destroy a family and inspiring them to live with character and conviction.